# VOICES *of*
# STEPNEY

# VOICES *of*
# STEPNEY

## DEE GORDON

*To Jonathan Gordon, son of Martin and Gail,*
*who died so suddenly during the writing of this book*

First published 2010

The History Press
The Mill, Brimscombe Port
Stroud, Gloucestershire, GL5 2QG
www.thehistorypress.co.uk

British Library Cataloguing in Publication Data.
A catalogue record for this book is available from the British Library.

ISBN 978 0 7524 5263 0

Typesetting and origination by The History Press
Printed in India, Aegean Offset
Manufacturing managed by Jellyfish Print Solutions Ltd

# CONTENTS

# INTRODUCTION

While the whole Western world saw a social and cultural revolution in the 1950s and '60s, London's East End probably saw more than most. This book focuses on Stepney (defined here as E1), recovering from the devastations of the wartime Blitz, a place being rebuilt for Cockneys and immigrants alike.

Meeting so many people who were a part of this living history has reinforced personal memories of the '50s, when material acquisition was not an everyday aspiration. One of the reasons that so many could, and did, leave their doors unlocked was because there was nothing to steal! It is only with hindsight that there is any sense of deprivation.

The higher earning power and access to increased social benefits of the '60s resulted in luxuries such as washing machines, which were 'saved up' for rather than being paid for with 'hire purchase'. The estates which so many locals moved into may have looked out of place, but were an improvement on the crowded, damp and often overcrowded dwellings they replaced, although less successful socially.

*Dee Gordon, 2010*

# CHARLIE BORG

## *Special Roots and Special Boots*

The surname Borg is Maltese, and Charlie's dad came over to England before the war. After a number of years as a stoker in the merchant navy, he moved to the Ministry of Works in the City, looking after their boilers, plus a later stint working on the cranes in Fair Trade Wharf. During the 1950s and '60s, the family, based in a terraced three-bedroom house in Caroline Street, grew to four boys (including Charlie) and four girls; one girl was sadly killed in a tragic accident in Cable Street in 1948.

As for Charlie, he was also unlucky enough to have been involved in a childhood accident which he was too young to remember, but which left him with a permanently damaged hip and leg. Instead of the local primary school, he was sent to a special residential school for disabled children in Surrey. He has happy memories of this school, and even happier ones of school holidays spent at home.

*King Edward Memorial Park (Shadwell Park), c.1969. (Courtesy of Tower Hamlets Local History Library)*

As a schoolboy, he and his brothers and E1 friends enjoyed building camps on bomb sites, laying booby traps in such places as Shadwell Park for unsuspecting passers-by, smuggling into the Troxy cinema (one brother needing to go in first to gain access), and even occasionally raiding the warehouse at the end of the street. None of these activities did any real harm, though there was the occasional brush with the law – as when a parachute from this warehouse (smuggled out with a couple of tents) was trailed down the street, attracting police attention. Result? A ticking off and their booty confiscated. Certainly, Charlie's callipers and stacked boot did not affect his ability or willingness to be 'one of the lads'.

At odds with this, perhaps, were Charlie's Sundays during the holidays, when he was an altar boy at St Mary's and St Michael's. There were Maltese masses at this church on Sunday afternoons, given in Maltese by a Maltese priest, and, because of the family connection, Charlie was roped into attending these, too. Many Maltese immigrants settled locally, some of them associated with local brothels, including one in Caroline Street.

Quite a lot, it seems, went on in Shadwell Park to amuse the local children. Its green riverside location was used in several films of the '50s – *The Long Haul* (released 1957) with Diana Dors and Victor Mature, the latter remembered by Charlie not for his film-star looks but for his habit of vehement spitting! Another film, *The Square Ring* (1953) actually featured Caroline Street, and another involved Barbara Windsor. When collecting autographs from the cast of *The Square Ring*, Charlie showed them to his mother, who was particularly amused by one signature which

*Troxy cinema, 2009. (Dee Gordon)*

*St George's Baths, c. 1969. (Courtesy of Tower Hamlets Local History Library)*

Charlie couldn't decipher: it read Rigor Mortis. He also remembers David McCallum filming part of *Violent Playground* (1958) in the Church of St Mary's and St Michael's.

Charlie was a scout both at home (the 8th Stepney Scouts) and in Surrey. Saturday morning pictures at the Troxy were quite an event, as they would usually have the bonus of a talent contest. For taking part in the contest, all entrants would have a free ticket for the following week, and Charlie remembers one brother singing a Christmas song in the middle of the summer which the audience were not at all keen on, but he got his ticket. Towards the end of the '50s, Charlie caught a glimpse of Cliff Richard going through the stage door of the Troxy, but this was not an event when it was possible to sneak in for nothing.

In 1959, Charlie was freed from his callipers and sent home from the Surrey school, his condition being monitored by visits on the train to the Queen Mary Hospital in Roehampton, the other side of London. His experiences at his local secondary school, Bishop Challoner for Boys in Hardinge Street, were less happy. The head was an ex-army tank commander who had no sympathy for Charlie, and insisted that he somersault over the horse like everyone else, which resulted in a painful landing on his hip. His fellow students were nearly as bad, stealing his belongings and running away, knowing that Charlie, in his raised shoe, could not keep up with them.

At home, life was much happier, in spite of such food as pigs' trotters and offal, and Charlie also remembers one of his sisters being sent to a nearby butcher's factory to buy a few

*The Borg family pre-1950. From right to left: Mum Ella, Charlie, sister Jean, sister Betty (d. 1948). (Charlie Borg collection)*

pence-worth of bones to make into stew or soup. His father raised chickens which he bought at Club Row market, and had as many as 500 in their scullery at one time. As he had trained as a butcher in his home country, he knew how to prepare chickens for the Christmas markets, and he usually slit their throats as his preferred form of slaughter. On one occasion, however, he chopped off a chicken's head, and the headless chicken ran into the street and was chased by the local children until it keeled over.

When in Club Row on Sundays with the family, Charlie's dad also bought up bits of bicycles, and brought them home to make up into 'new' bikes, with the help of his children. The children then rode the bikes back to Club Row to be sold – a successful sale meaning that you had to walk home.

During the school holidays, the staff from the iron foundry in nearby Pitsea Street played football in their lunch hour with the local boys. They even went to the trouble of making a 'proper' metal cup for the winners.

Christmases at home were dominated by Charlie's father and his friends from the docks who would arrive in Caroline Street after a visit to the pub, suitably lubricated, and with handfuls of coins which they threw on the floor for the Borg children. One brother, warned again and again that he would only get a sack of coal because he had been so naughty, was surprised to find that that was exactly what was waiting for him on Christmas Day, although his parents had concealed something for later in the day – they just needed to teach him a lesson.

The pawn-broker was a regular port of call – Fish's in Commercial Road. Even Charlie's suit would be pawned on occasion if funds were that short. The family also borrowed money from the loan clubs which were run at the local pubs. They managed to find the few pence necessary for the occasional use of the public baths in Bett Street, and Charlie also enjoyed a few visits to St George's Baths in The Highway, swimming being the only sport he really felt confident with.

It seems that the rag-and-bone man would take old china in exchange instead of hard cash, so when a whole stash of plates was found on a bomb site near to Dr Barnardo's in The Highway, it is not surprising that he and his sister loaded up a push-chair with the crockery, which came in very handy.

At least Charlie did not have to worry too much where his next pair of trousers was coming from – his granddad had a tailor's shop in Leman Street on the edge of the City. He had managed to secure a contract to make uniforms for the local police stations.

When the family finally moved out into what seemed like 'a palace' in Dagenham in the early '60s, everything was loaded into an open-backed lorry, with all the local children watching. As soon as they had left, a brick went straight through the window, but this was not personal, this was just 'fun' for those left behind.

# MIKE BOWYER
## AND SARAH STRINGER

*Still Pals ...*

Although Mike and Sarah were at primary school together in the early '60s, they tell different stories of growing up in Stepney.

Mike was born in Head Street near St Dunstan's Church, but the family had moved into a large flat in Welstead House in Ponler Street by 1961. His sister attended Harry Gosling's nursery before starting at the primary school (which had, exotically, a Japanese teacher), but Mike's mum seemed to want to keep him at home as long as possible, so he missed out on that experience. She did local cleaning jobs and worked as a child minder, later working in a pub in Bigland Street – the Australian Arms. His dad was a white-collar worker in the docks, also earning extra money at the Australian Arms.

This work ethic seems to have paid off, because the Bowyers had an Austin Cambridge A55 in 1961, a new model with plastic covers on the seats – covers which were not removed for around five years. A radiogram also arrived in the '60s, and Mike's dad would often come home with unexplained luxuries such as salted almonds and packs of toothbrushes.

The Welstead House flat was equipped with washing machine and communal wash room, and they had a television where Mike could watch his favourite programme – *Thunderbirds*. When anyone came calling who seemed a likely candidate to be checking on their television licence, the set was promptly taken out on to the balcony, covered by a blanket and topped with the parrot cage. The family also had a poodle called Chico, who didn't spend much time outside the flat – possibly because such pets were not 'allowed'. Generally, for Mike, life at home was sociable and fulfilling, with family card- and board-games.

In 1963, Mike's younger brother was born – at home – meaning that Mike had to be shipped out of the flat until it was all over. There were plenty of options open as the Bowyers had many family members living nearby, several in the resplendent-sounding Langdale Mansions. 'Nanny Crump' (his great-grandmother) lived off Ben Jonson Road, and she and several aunts would merit a visit most weekends, with Mike collecting 6d from each one. This money, together with his 2s 6d pocket money, meant he could buy his favourite Corgi toys and Airfix kits in the toy shop in Hessel Street, sweets (e.g. sherbet dabs) and Tizer from Jack Lerners in Burslem Street, and weekly copies of *Beezer*, *Hornet*, *Beano* and *Dandy*. He would also bring back bits of discarded prams and bicycles from the bomb sites to turn into go-karts which could be used down the hill by the railway, avoiding the main road at the bottom.

*Mike and sister Gillian, c. 1961. (Mike Bowyer collection)*

Football was a favourite with Mike and his dad, and, as a small boy, he sat on his dad's shoulders to watch the legendary Stanley Matthews playing at West Ham. Because he was at the back of the main stand, however, he could only see a small strip of turf, and didn't see too much of his hero. When West Ham beat Preston in the 1964 Cup Final, and when England won the World Cup in 1966, the Bowyer household indulged in great celebrations. Mike's dad made his elation clear to the neighbours by running up and down the balcony, making plenty of noise with his wooden football rattle. Fishing was a popular pursuit, with a canal close by, and Victoria Park not far away.

For Sarah, these early years were very different. She was brought up in a terraced house in Settles Street with her parents and younger sister. They used the two lower storeys including the basement, and her grandparents (who rented the house from the London Hospital) had the upper storeys. The bathroom was a tin bath in front of the fire in the living room on Sunday evenings, with the *Black-and-White Minstrels* or *Sing Something Simple* on the 'wireless'. There was an Ascot heater in the kitchen so that the girls' hair could be washed leaning over the kitchen sink.

Because her parents had moved to East London from different roots, they had no family nearby, and nowhere for the girls to run to when their dad was violent. He, too, brought home luxuries (a Moffat cooker for one) but didn't attempt to explain such windfalls. Her mum worked as a finisher locally, and her father was a diesel mechanic – often unemployed. Although dolls did not feature in her childhood, books did greatly. That's where any pocket money went, and that's what she wanted for Christmases and birthdays, building up a collection of hard-back classics (from such outlets as Whitechapel High Street, i.e. The Waste) including *I-Spy* books and even a full set of Arthur Mee's *Encyclopedia*. Books, it seems, formed an escape from the reality of Settles Street.

Every weekend in the street there was violence, especially from the houses on the other side of the road whose different coloured doors denoted private ownership. The West Indian families liked to have loud parties and the Asian families favoured gambling, which often flared up into violence. It was more entertaining to look out of the window on Friday or Saturday night than watch Gene Barry in *Burke's Law* on the television. Sarah also remembers that the Asian families who moved into these houses – which had inside toilets – actually removed and dumped the toilets as an undesirable facility.

School was a safe haven for Sarah (and her sister), and both Mike and Sarah have happy memories of their time at Harry Gosling – even though a tearful Mike ran away on his first day, promptly returned by his mum to a worried Miss Nugent who had been searching high and low for him. Sarah had the privilege of being a milk monitor, but she herself disliked the milk. This had usually been sitting in a crate for rather longer than it should have been and tasted warm to drink, putting her off the product for life.

She did like school dinners, though, as did Mike, and her mother worked as a school dinner lady for a while. There were two things that Mike did not like, however: runny custard and lumpy mashed potatoes. The school catered for the burgeoning Jewish population with a separate menu. When it came to school assembly, however, the Jewish children were not excluded – although Sarah noticed that they kept their hands behind their backs when it was time for prayers. The school celebrated Jewish as well as Christian festivals, e.g. Sukkot, at 'The Settlement' opposite the school premises, where greenery was rigged up overhead, and everyone was treated to orange and biscuits.

The two East Enders had different interests at school – Mike, following a game of kiss-and-chase on his second day, became enamoured with Maureen Camilleri who remained a long-term 'girlfriend'. Sarah joined Mr Reynolds' after-school photography club, which meant trips to such locales as Tower Hill, taking photos which were developed at school. They both collected stamps, however.

While Sarah was at home with her books, Mike was out playing football near Welstead House, until such time as there was no grass left to speak of – to the chagrin of the caretaker. There were plenty of bomb sites and opportunities for cycling and playing 'run-outs' (a bit like team tag) and you could buy bows and rubber-tipped arrows from the ironmongers in Ben Jonson Road to play cowboys and Indians. The only drawbacks in Mike's childhood were the constant visits to London Hospital at Whitechapel. He was born with a lazy eye and wore glasses (with plaster on one lens) from the age of two, with a need for regular checks.

They both remember bonfire nights and massive bonfires on the local bomb site near Langland Mansions (once the derelict, and unsafe, building on it was pulled down), such occasions being attended by large crowds who would bake potatoes on the fire's embers. Mike's parents would buy him the largest box of standard fireworks in the shop, and he and his 'gang' would also tie Catherine wheels to local saplings. Sarah and her sister would make their own guy which they would sit beside, outside their house, in the hope that enough passers-by would give them pennies.

*Mike at his nan's home in Donoghue Cottages, c. 1961. (Mike Bowyer collection)*

Sarah also recalls swimming at Goulston Street baths at Aldgate during weekends or summer holidays, which cost the princely sum of 6*d*. Any money not spent on books would go on records, and, as the '60s progressed, she became a fan of American tan nylons from local market stalls for 1*s* 11*d*. Whitechapel market was also the place to buy the model historical figures that interested her, which she painted as authentically as possible. On Sundays, she went to St Augustine's Church, and, every May Ascension Day, the church arranged a trip to Southend with a packed lunch – a day which she associates with endless rain.

Like Mike, she enjoyed Saturday morning pictures at the ABC in Mile End Road, a 2*d* bus ride away. For Mike, the morning would start with pie and (non-lumpy) mash at Watney Street Market, an interesting choice of breakfast. The cinema had its own chorus, which went something like this:

> Every Saturday we all line up,
> To see the films we like
> And shout aloud with glee.
> We like to laugh and have a sing song,
> Such a happy crowd are we.
> We are all pals together
> Minors of the ABC.

As for holidays, Mike's were mainly spent hop-picking in Kent. Two smells live on – the lovely smell of fresh hops, and the disgusting smell of the rotten ones. The children were paid by the parents to contribute to the picking, which was generally enjoyable, if hard work, in spite of the ear-wigs which fell off the vines, and in spite of the shabby huts they slept in. The pennies that Mike and his sister Gillian earned paid for treats such as cider lollies. Sarah's holidays were usually spent in a caravan in the St Osyth area, or camping in Epping Forest.

For Mike, food featured fairly prominently in his formative years, and he talked nostalgically of pickled herrings for Sunday tea, and cream cakes topped with fruit from the Jewish bakers in Hessel Street. Similarly, the Sir John Falstaff pub next to the railway bridge had a tiny off-licence that sold saveloys, and the combination of the smell of beer and saveloys brings it all back. Then there were the oranges dipped in sugar dished up by his grandma as a treat …

The end of the '60s was the end of their time at Harry Gosling, and effectively – in both cases – the end of their Stepney existence. Mike was offered the opportunity of a place at Westminster City School and started there a few weeks late (late 1967) because the family had booked their first trip abroad (to Majorca, from Luton airport) to coincide with the start of the first term. This late start hampered him not only for his first year but for his subsequent years there, which he puts down to 'feeling sorry for himself'. While there, until his dad was made redundant and took over a pub in Old Street (London EC1) in 1969, he still socialised with his Stepney friends, although homework now took up a good part of his spare time.

At the age of just ten, Sarah won a scholarship to Greycoats School (coincidentally, also in Westminster), but she never got there. Her dad left the family home, so she and her mum and sister moved near to her grandmother in Solihull, where she spent her last school years.

# ELSIE BROTHERTON

## *Living Over the Shop*

Commercial Road was the centre of Elsie's life in the 1950s and '60s. She had married her second husband Charlie in 1951 at the East End Mission (also in Commercial Road), a man with a busy business – Brotherton & Sons. Brotherton's provided iron and steel essentials for the fishing trade and other elements of the catering industry. For example, the metal baskets and boilers for crabs were sold not just to fishermen but to large-scale buyers at Billingsgate Fish Market, then in the City. Over the road was her parents' wet fish shop, Lagsden's.

Elsie and Charlie lived in the flat over the business, premises owned by the railway, which had been reduced in size after much of the lead had been removed from its roof during the war. Elsie had been used to a bigger house with her first husband, but put up with the lack of space, with having to use the public baths in Cable Street and with working hard seven days per week. The baths, incidentally, had male and female attendants to top up the hot water: Mrs Downer for the ladies and Tom Tucker for the men.

*Commercial Road, 1952. (Courtesy of Tower Hamlets Local History Library)*

*Brotherton's shop, late 1960s. (Elsie Brotherton collection)*

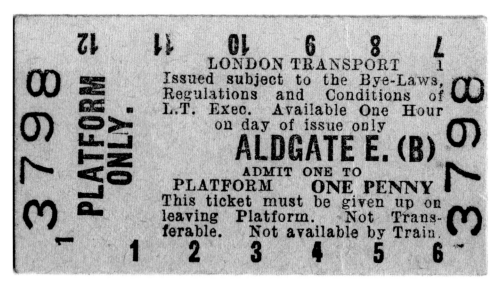

*Aldgate tube ticket, 1957. (Dee Gordon collection)*

Just as her own mother helped her husband in his fish shop, so Elsie helped Charlie with his business, and she learned to drive partly to make it easier for her to make essential trips to and from the warehouse. Charlie was out every night for a drink in his favourite local, Holland's, in Exmouth Street, but Elsie accepted this as part of his way of life, although she wasn't so keen when he brought people home at closing time, especially if they expected to be fed. If she felt the need for a night out, she would sometimes accompany her parents to the Swan, which was their preferred watering hole, although the birth of son David in 1954 made even this difficult.

Apart from summer Sundays at a caravan in Hullbridge (near Southend), Elsie lived quite a narrow existence and feels that life, for her, didn't begin until the '70s. This was when she inherited a bungalow at Pitsea (Essex) from her mother, which she sold in order to buy a house in Westgate-on-Sea in Kent where she still lives. It was also the time she saw an advertisement for GPO telephonists and decided (aged fifty-three) to apply. She was taken on and trained in Brick Lane, going on to work in the City and then in Westgate, after David had his formative education at Sir John Cass School at Aldgate.

Elsie's brother Bill (Lagsden) and sister-in-law Ann, who lived in Barnes Street in the '50s, have their own claim to fame. They were contestants on *Beat the Clock* at the London Palladium at the time Bruce Forsyth was 'in charge' and won some worthwhile prizes to take home to Barnes Street.

# BARRY AND SHEILA BROWN

*Rising Above Life's Disadvantages*

Barry was brought up in what he describes as 'an English prefab' in Braintree Street. This was one of the white box-like post-war constructions with a black roof, the front door opening into the 'front room' which, in spite of the open fire, was always cold in the winter. The prefab was shared with his older sister, Brenda, mum Alice and dad Harry.

Harry Brown was a lorry driver with Charrington's Brewery in Mile End Road right through the '50s and '60s and beyond. His wife did occasional office cleaning, including a stint at the nearby John Scurr Primary School. Regular visitors to Braintree Street were the ice-cream man on a motorbike with a side-car, who would regularly ask Barry's mum for a glass of 'Adam's Ale'. There was also a man-in-a-van who sold iced biscuits and roasted peanuts door-to-door, and the fish and cockles man on Sunday afternoons.

An early memory is of his first day at Cephas Street Infant School, when Miss Elliot told Alice that Barry should be in a special school because he had had a stroke in infancy, leaving a weakness on the left side. Alice Brown was not so easily foisted off, and insisted that he could manage perfectly well at Cephas – which he did. Whether this was due to the tablespoonful of malt dished out every day is debatable – the fact that everyone used the same spoon would not have gone down too well with today's Health & Safety police, that's for sure.

His sister was then at John Scurr Primary but, when she passed her Eleven Plus, she went to a grammar school in Clapton, E5. Soon after (1953) was the year that the Browns went up in the world when they bought their first twelve-inch black and white Murphy television for £80, in time for the Coronation. Barry also remembers that this was the year that Stanley Matthews was in the cup final, and quite a few neighbours without televisions came in to watch the match. As for the Coronation itself, there was a street party in Braintree Street, with a stage, on which young Barry – dressed appositely as a crown – came second in the fancy dress contest.

His dad's favourite locals were the Essex Arms in Braintree Street, and the Woolpack. Mr and Mrs Brown also frequented the Toby Club for Charrington's staff in Whitehead Street. Here there were dances, plus parties for the children and outings organised by coach to ice shows and pantomimes.

When it came to the Browns' turn to be re-housed, his parents were not at all happy with either the flat or the estate they were offered, in Hackney. It took the help of Solly Kaye, the local Communist MP, to arrange a preferable move to the much newer Ocean Estate in Mile End Road, along with many neighbours and friends. They were lucky enough to secure a three-bedroom terraced cottage in Shandy Street, where houses surrounded a square with a green in the middle. The square became an unofficial football pitch, and a local lad, David, is a friend of Barry's to this day.

*Charrington's Beano. Outside brewery, Harry in centre with cigarette in mouth. (Barry Brown collection)*

*Charrington's Beano from Bancroft Estate, Harry is bottom right. (Barry Brown collection)*

*Coronation party outside John Scurr School. (Barry Brown collection)*

Barry's next school was Ben Jonson when it was comparatively new (1956/1957), a bright school with a large playground ideal for football or boxing at play-time. Barry's education was partially disrupted when he started travelling twice a week to St Thomas's Hospital in Westminster for physiotherapy. Before that, he had been having twice-yearly checkups at Mile End Hospital, but Alice Brown was not happy that this was enough, and persuaded the specialist, Dr Phillips, to increase the therapy that she felt her son needed. Barry feels this made a real difference and was grateful that it was available, in spite of the twenty-minute tube ride each way.

Barry enjoyed spending his money on comics (*Beano* and *Dandy*) and swapping them for others once he had read them from cover to cover. There were plenty of local bomb sites to play on, and on Saturday mornings he could see *Flash Gordon* or *Davy Crockett* at the ABC cinema in Mile End Road. In 1958, he saw his first live football match with his dad – at Leyton Orient. A few years later, when he got to travel with his friends, he reminisces that you could get a train to Leyton or Tottenham, pay for the entrance and the programme, and all for 'half a crown' (12.5p).

The family had a car from the early 1950s, with a motorbike and side-car before that. At one point as a youngster he and his cousin managed to get themselves locked into the side-car, and it had to be forced open, not pleasing his dad too much. When his dad brought the brewery's lorry home at lunch-time and parked up outside the prefab, Barry (often accompanied by a friend) would amuse himself 'mucking about with the wires under the dashboard' while Harry Brown had his dinner. Inevitably, on one occasion a fire damaged the controls, which needed the know-how of a brewery mechanic to repair – luckily, this was Alice Brown's cousin …

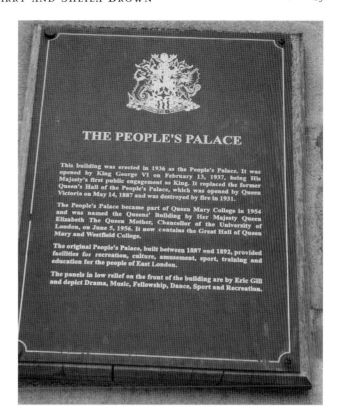

*People's Palace plaque. (Dee Gordon)*

His next school was Morpeth Secondary Modern in Bethnal Green, where he also became involved with the Stewart Headlam Club, a youth club set up for the school's pupils. There was also Repton Boys' Club – also in Bethnal Green – which gave the boys somewhere to go after school, and which was a particularly good venue for snooker. There is one particular school prize-giving that sticks in his mind – the time when Clement Attlee gave out the prizes at the People's Palace in Mile End Road. His visits to the hospital were cut to once a week at Morpeth, partly due to some improvement in his flexibility and partly to avoid jeopardising his education. Near to the school, Barry remembers the distinctive smell of Bilinders, a confectionery factory in Bancroft Road – he can't recall the sweets, just the smell.

By now, incidentally, Brenda, his sister, had left school and was working as a wages clerk for Miller's (engineering) in Brick Lane. She was married in 1961 at St Dunstan's Church with a large wedding reception at Dame Collett Hall, and moved with her husband to Bethnal Green.

In the 1950s and '60s Marion Richardson School in Senrab Street, Stepney, held a yearly summer fête which was very popular locally. The fête was normally opened and attended by celebrities of the period. In the early '60s Barry and his mother and Brenda (who was pregnant at the time with her first daughter) went to visit the fête, which was opened that day by the singer Marion Ryan and Leslie Crowther. It seems that Leslie Crowther made a point of very kindly wishing Brenda good luck with her future 'happy event', a gesture which particularly impressed Mrs Brown.

*Barbara Windsor and James Booth in* Sparrows Can't Sing. *(Dee Gordon collection)*

On Sunday mornings, Barry could be seen down Brick Lane, standing outside the pub with his comics while his dad had a drink with his granddad – although dad usually favoured the Bancroft Arms. Granddad lived in Great Eastern Buildings in Cheshire Street, and liked to treat himself to a hot sasparilla (or sarsaparilla) drink from one of the stalls. Brick Lane was also the place where the Browns bought all their shoes – in Blackman's, with Chaplin's in Bethnal Green Road the place for made-to-measure suits once he was working.

After Morpeth, Barry's first job was with Brown and Tawse in Bromley-by-Bow, but he only stayed a few months because his dad managed to find him a job at Charrington's in the Transport Office. This job lasted for four years, when he moved on to William Massey's, the bookies, where he did a course in turf accountancy. For the rest of the '60s, he worked mainly in their Stepney Green shop.

Memories of the Ocean Estate are of the lifts in the flats which stank of coal dust from the coal deliveries, and of a neighbour's daughter being run over by a milk float in the square outside their house. As a witness, Alice Brown was nervous at the time about getting someone into 'trouble' over what she had seen. Her sister also moved on to the estate, and the families had holidays in sea-side resorts such as Great Yarmouth.

In February 1963, the premiere of *Sparrows Can't Sing*, which had been filmed locally, was held at the ABC in Mile End Road. Barry recalls the crowds of people waiting outside who had come along not only to get a peek at the film's stars (Barbara Windsor, James Booth, George Sewell, and Stephen Lewis) and Joan Littlewood (the director) but other visiting stars such as Richard Todd, Stanley Baker, Charlie Drake, Arthur Askey and Miriam Karlin. The Metropolitan Police Band and the trumpeters from the Household Cavalry were also there to entertain the crowds, although, disappointingly, Princess Margaret – billed to attend – was 'indisposed' so the only royal to be seen was the Earl of Snowdon. Even so, Wally's tea-bar was unceremoniously moved from his regular pitch outside for the duration, perhaps with the 'help' of the Krays – acquaintances of Barbara Windsor – who were also in evidence.

Barry passed his driving test in 1965, and was able to borrow his dad's old Ford Prefect to go to such places as the Tottenham Royal on a Saturday night, or to see live acts such as Rod Stewart or Long John Baldry at Manor House. A year or so later, he got himself a Volkswagen Beetle from a Plaistow dealers, for the princely sum of £270. Otherwise, his money went on records (his first 45 was *Let there be Drums* by Sandy Nelson which cost 4s 3d) – mainly from Petticoat Lane or from Wally for Wireless who had a stall outside Whitechapel station on Saturdays. Plus there were plenty of local pubs to spend money in of course – Kate 'Odders, the Rose and Punchbowl and the Aberdeen, or the Green Gate in Bethnal Green.

Barry's wife, Sheila, is also from Stepney. She was living in Cleveland Way until slum clearance in the '50s saw her also re-located to the Ocean Estate. Her memories of the period and the area are similar to Barry's, except for the fact that she was brought up as a Roman Catholic, attending St Anne's School in Underwood Road and then St Gregory the Great in Bethnal Green. She was not too impressed by the frequency of mass at St Anne's or the strict regime imposed at St Gregory's – although the processions, particularly those on St Patrick's Day, were happier times.

# STAN BULLMAN

### *Altar Boy ... And Mod*

An only child, Stan lived with his mum and dad in Dunelm Street, with an aunt downstairs, right through the 1950s until 1966. His primary school was St Mary's and St Michael's in Heckford Street, and his teachers were sisters of mercy, with Sister Cyril at the helm. He remembers free school milk in little bottles in the '50s and a disgusting cheese-and-egg pie served up regularly for school dinners – and he also recalls that this school was used for the filming of *To Sir With Love* (with Lulu) in the '60s.

As for his home, the family lived in one room where eating, cooking and washing all took place, with two very cold bedrooms. To boost bed-time warmth, his parents added their old ARP warden coats as extra bedding in lieu of quilts. In the absence of a bathroom, his mum made use of his aunt's bathroom, and Stan used the public baths in Jamaica Street. These baths were not only noisy, but, because of the demand, he was always being told to 'hurry up' so that it was more of a chore than a pleasure. Stan's father worked for the Ministry of Works as a pipe fitter, so they did have the benefit of an Ascot heater for hot water. His mother made ladies' shoes for a Hackney manufacturer.

Both his parents were happy to stay at home with each other for company. Dad was a Barnardo's boy, well trained in such domestic chores as bed-making, and very much head of the family. They encouraged young Stan to attend St Mary's and St Michael's Church regularly (twice on Sundays), and Stan was an altar boy from an early age. The highlight of the church year was the annual procession when the local roads were closed off. When he was a bit older, there was a Catholic club after church on Sundays, the Vaughan Club.

As a youngster, he and local friends liked street games, playing football, and visiting Victoria Park Lido in good weather. During the school holidays, he stayed with his aunt who lived nearby, her three boys making ideal playmates. He didn't have any holidays with his parents, though they did go hop-picking a few times in Kent, utilising his uncle's lorry to get there and back. Holidays came in the '60s with friends, usually to the Isle of Wight.

On Saturday mornings, the Troxy in Commercial Road was a favourite of Stan's. He particularly remembers being fascinated by the world yo-yo champion, one Art Pickles, who visited the venue one Saturday, and ran a yo-yo competition, which Stan was delighted to win. At Christmas, he would look forward to such delights as a compendium of board games, stuffed into a pillowcase in the absence of a stocking. His dad was quite handy at making things, and would be able to produce such wonders as a hand-made scooter. The Christmas holiday would be spent with his grandparents in a council flat on the Ocean Estate.

In 1956, Stan began attending a Catholic grammar school in Blackheath – St Joseph's Academy – a sought after placement. This involved him walking to Shadwell station, getting a

*Stan and his parents, c. 1950.*
*(Stan Bullman collection)*

*Stan as an altar boy in St Mary's*
*and St Michael's. (Stan Bullman*
*collection)*

*Stan (left) in a church procession. (Stan Bullman collection)*

*Tubby Isaacs' stall. (Courtesy of Tubby Isaacs)*

tube to New Cross, and then a main-line train to Blackheath; quite a trek for an eleven-year-old twice a day. He played rugby for the school and joined an East London club called Fairbairn House. One attraction of playing rugby was the use of the showers.

On leaving school at sixteen, he took on a five-year apprenticeship as a compositor in Shoreditch. He had always been good at English, and a fan of John Bull Printing sets. He cycled to and from his job, moving on to other printing companies when he'd finished his apprenticeship, and eventually achieved his aim of getting into Fleet Street.

Stan's early earnings were spent on records played on a radiogram borrowed from his aunt downstairs, and he liked shoes, and Mod outfits. Most of his Mod clothes he bought in Carnaby Street, but there was a shop in the Mile End Road (Albert's) where you could pick up the essential polo shirts. The pubs he frequented were favourites with local Mods, principally Kate 'Odders (as it was known) on the Ocean Estate, where the Small Faces had played live and were said to have been inspired by the local park to write one of their most famous songs – 'Itchycoo Park' – though it has other claims for its source. Other Mod haunts were the Fountain in Mile End Road, the Rose and Punchbowl, the Blind Beggar, the Ship, and the George Tavern in Commercial Road.

For live music, Stan would go 'up West' to such haunts as the Marquee in Wardour Street, and remembers the Two I's Coffee Bar in Old Compton Street (the birthplace of British Rock 'n' Roll), and dancing at the Strand Lyceum all day Sunday. He was also part of the large groups that would descend on such seaside resorts as Southend-on-Sea in the summer to pose along the promenade on their Lambrettas or Vespas – but he was always a passenger, not a driver.

He met his first wife at Our Lady's Hall, a mixed social club over the Vaughan Club. They married at St Mary's and St Michael's, but soon moved out to Essex, where Stan remains to this day. But he can still remember the smell of the bagels from Goldring's Jewish bakery in Commercial Road on Sundays and the taste of real pie and mash and Tubby Isaacs' jellied eels.

*The Blind Beggar, 2009. (Dee Gordon)*

# THE FRANKS FAMILY

## *Part of a Community*

Doreen Franks and her parents spent the 1950s and '60s in Brokesley Street in Bow, just over the Stepney border, but a lot of their time was spent in Stepney. They had relatives living in Turner Street, opposite the nurses' home for London Hospital, and spent many hours visiting, shopping and socialising in E1.

Aunt Eve in Turner Street lived in a tall, terraced house with a basement, shared with friends. The youngest son at this household, Michael, had a Meccano set and Doreen liked playing with this when they went to visit. Everyone liked to visit on Sunday morning, particularly as you could also buy fresh bagels and pretzels nearby.

Stepney shopping at that time, especially on Sundays, focused mainly on food. Mossy Marks in Wentworth Street was a favourite for smoked salmon, plus the sauerkraut and barrels of smoked herrings in which you could dip your hand and pull out your lunch. Outside, at least two ladies in opposition to each other would try and persuade you to buy some of the bagels they sold from their baskets, vying for your attention and shouting insults at each other. The Franks would buy salt beef at Barnett's in Middlesex Street, the same butcher's that Doreen's grandmother (from Frying Pan Alley) and great-grandmother used. As an alternative, there was Strongwater's in Mile End Road whose salt beef sandwiches were particularly good. Further afield, in Commercial Street, there was a cake shop with rickety old stairs (Monnikendams) whose specialism was Stuffed Monkey Cake, which apparently tasted better than it sounds.

On Fridays, Hessel Street Market (near Watney Street) specialised in supplying the local Jewish immigrants, and it was rare to hear any language other than Yiddish spoken there. There was a stall with kosher chickens complete with heads and feathers hanging on butcher's hooks. After choosing your chicken and haggling over the price, it would be hooked down with a pole and the head cut off. For 2d extra, you could hand your chicken to the 'flicker' and this very well-muscled lady who sat on an up-turned orange-box with sacking on her lap would de-feather your bird.

There were dances at weekends at Stepney Youth Club in Beaumont Grove, usually with live music or sometimes a disco. Doreen recalls making coffee at the club for Bert Weedon – before he became a big name. This club also organised evening classes after school for art and drama, with the addition of table tennis and similar indoor activities for local Jewish teenagers. One particular painting in art class involved stamping your feet in paint before transferring it to the canvas. However, Doreen has a certificate (1961) for one of her more sedate artistic efforts – a vista of trees.

Around 1955, there was a bit of excitement in Whitechapel Road when Wally for Wireless opened – because Wally had invited Frankie Vaughan to do the honours. Doreen went along

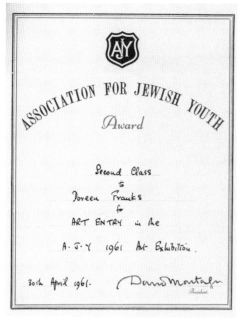

*Doreen's certificate for artwork. (Doreen Franks collection)*

*Wally for Wireless, 1961. (Courtesy of Tower Hamlets Local History Library)*

with her mother (Annie) and her friend Janet, along with hundreds of other screaming fans, but the shop was so crowded it was difficult to get more than a glimpse of their hero. Janet missed him altogether because she fainted in all the excitement, narrowly escaping being badly injured in the crush, and ended up in the London Hospital over the road. Annie Franks recalls that he 'was much smaller than he looks on the television'!

Although Doreen went to secondary school in E2 (Morpeth), she recalls attending workshops at Toynbee Hall (Commercial Street) in the sixth form. Ben Jonson's play *Bartholomew Fair* was being rehearsed, and the Morpeth students were able to attend for a number of consecutive days to see how the whole thing was put together. When she left school a few years later and went to Brentwood to train as a teacher, she was not a residential student, and in the evenings would go to classes at Myrdle Street School alongside London Hospital in Whitechapel. As a student, funds to buy clothes were limited, so Doreen learned dress making, and went on to make all her own clothes (using fabrics from Paul's in Petticoat Lane) including a tailored tweed jacket and a trendy jumpsuit.

Stepney Green Synagogue in Rectory Square played quite a prominent role in the Jewish communities in Stepney and surrounding areas. Doreen went to a couple of weddings there in the 1950s and '60s (the Hotel Central in Mansell Street, Aldgate, was 'the' place for receptions) and it was where her friend Vivienne married a Sephardic Indian at the end of the 1960s, a memorable occasion. It was also popular for bar mitzvahs. With its black-and-white marble interior, it seems that the synagogue was apparently – and a tad oddly – known as the Cathedral of the East End, and Doreen's uncle kept a numbered seat for which an annual fee was charged – it cost extra to have a front seat. This synagogue (among others) gave out annual

*The Franks at a family wedding, late 1950s. (Doreen Franks collection)*

Passover parcels for poorer local families which included matzos, smoked salmon, eggs, kosher margarine, salami, kosher tea, oil, and baklava (pastry), all donated by businesses, with extra parcels being donated for larger families.

Other memorable shops in the vicinity were the jeweller's shops. One in Black Lion Yard (off Whitechapel Road, but no longer in evidence) seemed to attract the Jewish population. Whole families would pack into this tiny shop to make significant purchases, i.e. the engagement ring and perhaps the wedding ring too. Spiegelhalters in Mile End Road (with Wickham's Department Store on either side) was another favourite, although Doreen ran out in the '50s when her mum took her to have her ears pierced, and didn't have the courage to go back and have it done until her twenty-first birthday in 1967.

When Doreen and her mum were not shopping at weekends, they were working. (Her father worked Saturdays, too, as part of his six-day week as a postman.) Doreen worked all day Saturday in Roman Road and Sunday mornings in Petticoat Lane for Dave Vernon who owned a couple of dress stalls – not just because she had a crush on his son, but because the money was handy. Annie worked Fridays and Saturdays in Roman Road market on either a

*The remains of Wickham's Department Store, 2009. (Dee Gordon)*

confectionery stall or a grocery stall, and on Sundays in Petticoat lane for Barnett's, a record stall (45s and 78s) where the records were demonstrated on a wind-up record player. The best selling records (apart from Elvis in the '50s and The Beatles in the '60s) were Joe Brown, Cliff Richard, Marty Wilde and Lonnie Donegan. At the end of the day, some of the unsold records were sold off cheaply.

In Cephas Street (which runs from Cambridge Heath Road to Globe Road) was Dr Collier's practice, the GP that Mr Franks favoured, because he had known him since they were young boys together. Dr Collier met his wife, a nurse, at the Jewish hospital in Stepney Green, and, in fact, this hospital attracted Jewish nurses and doctors from all over the UK. Having spent a lot of time there visiting elderly relatives, the impression it has left behind is of cleanliness and of tight controls. No sitting on the bed, only two visitors at a time, no children except at weekends, and patients confined to their bed when they had visitors. Visitors were not offered comfortable seating, just a hard bench that was pulled out from under the hospital bed; an austere façade, an austere set-up – but seemingly effective and much missed.

# DEE GORDON

## *The Author's Story*

As I, too, spent the 1950s and '60s in Stepney, it does not seem inappropriate to add my own account to all those who have given me their own stories.

The first house I lived in – 23 Leatherdale Street – was demolished, as was the whole street, in a slum clearance programme in 1958. It was a three-storey terraced house, with a family on each floor. At the beginning of the '50s, I was living on the ground floor in my pre-school days, an only child, with my mum and dad, who were both well into their forties.

We had three rooms – a bedroom for all three of us, a living room and a kitchen. There was a backyard, which was where the outside 'lav' was to be found. The kitchen, barely big enough for a table and chairs, was the room where we washed (stripped, in turn, over the kitchen sink), ate, listened to the radio, read library books and, in my mum's case, knitted. It was the only room with any heat, thanks to the tiny black stove with the coal fire alongside. A kettle was kept atop this fire pretty much all day every day as far as I recall.

The two beds were covered with outdoor coats for warmth, newspapers being added in the winter when I vividly remember the condensation every morning when I looked out into the barren yard. I would watch mum from this window as she took out armfuls of washing to what was little more than a shed; then she'd take out bowls of hot water, and wash everything by hand, hanging it out to dry on the washing line after using the mangle which was her pride and joy.

It astonishes me, looking back, that we had that third room, the living room, furnished with seating and a 'proper' wooden table and chairs, but which was used primarily for birthdays and Christmas. It had a fireplace but, again, the fire was only lit on the rare occasions when the room was in use. Perhaps the cost of the fire was just too much to contend with, but I can only guess. At the time, it all seemed perfectly normal, the room being kept for 'best'.

After a few years on the ground floor, the tenants on the first floor moved out, and we progressed upward. The first floor had two bedrooms and an indoor toilet, so this was a great improvement and, not only that, but we actually used the living room and its open fire on a regular basis. Dad – who worked most of his life as a cellarman for a Regent Street wine merchants – must have had a raise!

We still washed in the kitchen, though, but this time in a tin bath that was hauled down from the top of a cupboard. All mod cons indeed. There was certainly no sense of deprivation, and it was sheer bliss not to have to dash out into the yard every time you needed the toilet, especially during bad weather. My favourite memory of those years is of being woken every morning (in my very own bedroom) by the rag-and-bone man next door. The sound of his shire's hooves on the cobbles every morning was my alarm call, and, from my window, I watched horse and cart start their day. It was also a common sight to see shires pulling brewer's drays in the area.

Mum and dad, George and Dora Winston, c.1959.
(Dee Gordon collection)

Whitechapel Market, 1960s. (Courtesy of Tower
Hamlets Local History Library)

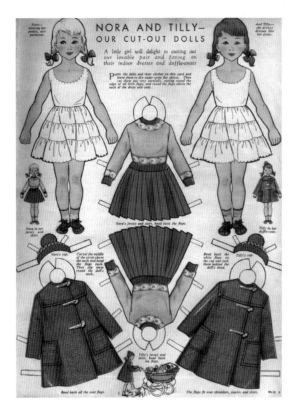

1950s paper dolls. (Dee Gordon collection)

The most abiding memory of the mid-'50s was the street party for the Coronation in 1953. All the local children dressed up and, rather oddly, my Union Jack top half was paired with a hula skirt. There must have been a reason at the time. The local mothers had gone to such a lot of trouble to provide sandwiches, jellies, fairy cakes and sausage rolls, and the whole street was set off with patriotic bunting, all of which must have been home-made. Everyone, it seems, without exception, was a royalist. Christmases in Leatherdale Street were always spent at home – apart from Christmas dinner which was at my mum's sister in Jamaica Street: she was a better cook than mum, had a bigger family, and a piano. My favourite gift at that age was always cut-out paper dolls, with cut-out clothes to dress them in. Cheap and cheerful maybe, but I loved them.

In 1958, we were offered a council flat less than half a mile away on the Bancroft Estate. We went to have a look at number 13 Bancroft House and were happy with what we saw – first floor with a lift, a balcony back and front, electric fires, and a proper bathroom with hot water on tap. We even had a proper cooker and a 'boiler' to do the washing, although Mum kept the mangle, which found a home on our tiny balcony overlooking the rear of Charrington's Brewery. This part of Stepney was closer to Whitechapel, and our neighbours were the Gibsons and the Rogoffs, orthodox Jewish families who asked us to switch off their lights on Fridays, and gave us gifts of matzos at fasting times. Young Trudi Gibson, next door at number 14, was a similar age to me, but lived a very different life – I recall her

*Prize giving at Morpeth (Dee front right),*
c. *1960. (Dee Gordon collection)*

perfectly-groomed auburn ringlets (reminiscent of Violet Elizabeth in *Just William*) and her pristine white apron that always protected her clothes if she should venture outside her front door onto the balcony to peer at the likes of me and the other local children playing in the concreted grounds of the flats.

I have to say I can't really recall much of a social life for any of us in the '50s. There was Saturday morning pictures for me, of course, dominated – it seems – by Westerns. The first film I went to see with Mum was *Snow White*, the first full-length Disney cartoon feature, at the ABC in Mile End Road – and I know I saw other films with her and sometimes even with Dad, too, but I have no recollection of what they were. Once a year, the council would organise an outing for us estate kids, but, again, I can remember just the one - Tommy Steele in *Half a Sixpence* at the London Palladium.

'Going out' didn't seem important when I was growing up. Dad would go to the local pub every Saturday evening and Sunday lunchtime, and sometimes Mum would join him on Saturday, which meant I had to wait outside with my packet of crisps and glass of lemonade – but I was watching the world go by, and it didn't seem such a bad life. On rainy Saturdays, the pub – the Globe in Globe Road, now derelict – had a tiny off-licence where I, sometimes with other local youngsters, would be able to hear the adults singing: my dad's favourite was 'Comrades' and I can still hear him sing it now.

Other than that, outings with Mum were to Roman Road market on Saturday mornings, often finishing up with lunch in the pie-and-mash-shop. (Oh, how I hated the white 'liquor'

*Mod style, Bancroft House balcony, c. 1964. (Dee Gordon collection)*

– with parsley – that they put on the plates, and it put me off mash ever after!) Saturday afternoons were sometimes spent looking around Wickham's Department Store in Mile End Road, though I don't think we ever bought anything, or a visit to Whitechapel market, known as The Waste. More often, it was the library as we were spoilt for choice – there was one in Bancroft Road, one in Whitechapel Road, and one in Bethnal Green Gardens, the nearest. (Mum read a Mills and Boon every day …) For an occasional treat, I loved looking at the elaborate dolls' houses in Bethnal Green Museum – but I never did get one of my own.

I think Dad was probably disappointed that I never developed an interest in his football team, Leyton Orient, or any football team come to that, because that is where he would spend his Saturday afternoons – I did accompany him a few times when very young, young enough to need to sit on his shoulders, but I remember the mounds of peanut shells we left behind us better than I remember the football. Dad was happily occupied at the weekend with his trips to the nearby betting shop in Cambridge Heath Road, his football pools – which commanded complete silence when the results were broadcast around tea-time on Saturdays – and he taught me to play cards (rummy, which I have since forgotten).

On Sunday mornings, we occasionally visited Petticoat Lane, stopping off at Tubby Isaacs' stall on the way back to buy winkles for Sunday tea. Often as not we would visit an aunt in the afternoon – there were plenty to choose from as Dad had fifteen brothers and sisters, and Mum had three sisters.

The only time we left Stepney was for a day-trip on the train to Southend (usually for the carnival) or for hop-picking (in the 1950s) when I have hazy recollections of lorry-loads of singing Cockneys and sleeping on the floor in a crowded hut; or the annual two-week holiday in August. In my case, it was to Ramsgate, to the same boarding house every year. The landlady, Nora, became like yet another aunt, and we enjoyed the familiarity of the return visits.

School for me was Cephas School (infants) in Cephas Street, John Scurr Primary, and Morpeth Secondary in Morpeth Street, over the 'border' in Bethnal Green. A particular memory from John Scurr was taking the leading role in a play called *Amahl and the Night Visitors*. This play was staged in a competition at York Hall in Bethnal Green, and we won! I was so pleased with myself, and not only that, but I had got to kiss Francis Joncock, my absolute favourite, who played my son, Amahl – well, okay, it was a mother-and-son type kiss, but still a kiss.

Because I had passed my Eleven Plus, I remember going to Raines Foundation Grammar for an interview, but when I chose the secondary modern where my friends were going, in preference, my teacher at John Scurr (Mr Griffin) was furious with me, telling me I'd end up as a cleaner 'like my mum'. Oh, those halcyon non-PC days! A few of the more dysfunctional teachers made a bit of an impression at Morpeth. There was the English teacher, who wore red lipstick in clown style, to match dyed red hair; the science teacher, who could be seen taking a quick snifter from a hip flask in his desk; the French teacher, who was so red-faced he glowed and who was completely unable to control any class; and the strict music teacher, who was always sending me out of the class to wash off make-up or change out of my stilettos! Again, I remember the school plays, where I always seemed to have the lead – mainly because I could remember the lines, I suspect – playing such roles as Pocahontas, or Titania (*Midsummer Night's Dream*).

My mum was indeed a cleaner, doing the early morning stint at offices in the City, but only because money was needed for my school uniform. Apart from that, she was a stay-at-home mum, the sort who always wore an apron, with a turban covering rollers in her hair, but who taught me to read before I started infant school and was always ready to lend a helping hand with homework.

Once I'd left school and was working and earning money in a variety of office jobs in the City, the '60s for me were pretty typical of teenagers everywhere. I went on holiday with friends to Butlin's at Clacton (where, in 1965, I met my first husband). I bought clothes from Biba's catalogue followed by rare visits to her store, as Kensington High Street was a bit of a trek. The nearest disco was a few miles north in Dalston – where I saw the Rolling Stones before they were famous; and the nearest 'palais' was at Leytonstone Town Hall – a mecca for East London Mods like me. My favourite Mod outfit, incidentally, was a full-length mustard suede coat with navy blue sleeves and collar, which I had made-to-measure in Petticoat Lane for a song – and wore everywhere, even on the dance floor …

The '60s club scene for me was mostly in the West End – the Scene on Monday, the Marquee on Wednesday, the Last Chance on Thursday, the Discotheque on Friday, and the Flamingo on Saturday night and Sunday afternoon, featuring the likes of Rod Stewart and Georgie Fame – without a drop of alcohol in sight, just a few 'blues' to keep you awake in the wee hours. I did spend the occasional evening in the Blind Beggar before it became notorious – but pubs were not really my scene. Stepney, it seems, had little to offer me at that point, but it is the backbone that has been with me all my adult life since moving out in the early '70s when I married. I will always be proud of my East End roots.

# MARTIN GORDON

## *Rag Trade and Rifles*

Martin and his family were living in slum clearance property by the outbreak of the Second World War. They were there throughout the 1950s in Felix House in Split Street, later re-named Forbes Street (near Cable Street), Martin only moving out when he got married in 1965.

The cramped Split Street flat had no kitchen to speak of and cooking often took place on their 'balcony' (a glamorous description of a miniscule outside 'space'), even utilising an open fire if the weather permitted. The family – there were six sons including Martin – managed with two bedrooms and without a bathroom or running water, although he does remember a small black 'oven' in the living area. His father had his own manufacturing business, Emanuel's, at the corner of the street, employing a couple of dozen machinists, and his mother, Polly, helped out when she could. The business was boosted to some extent by uniforms for the War Department.

In the 1950s, Martin was at St George's Central School, in Cable Street, a mixed school with a 'real gent of a headmaster' in Mr White. Martin's *bête noire* was woodwork on Friday afternoons, which took place at Harry Gosling School next door, and, when the class upped and moved from one base to the other, that was his opportunity to 'bunk off' and take himself to the public baths in Betts Street for his weekly clean up. For a bit of pocket money, he helped out the local milkman who was still delivering his wares with a horse and cart. Local Jewish boys' clubs kept him off the street after school – the Brady Club and, earlier, the Bernhard Baron Settlement.

Cable Street, 1956. (Rob Clack, Forum Casebook)

*National Service discharge notice. (Martin Gordon collection)*

The household was not a kosher one, although his mother was originally from an orthodox family, and they followed some customs, doing away with bread at Passover for example. Martin was not bar mitzvahed, although two of his brothers were, and he also missed out on Hebrew lessons at the synagogue which should have taken place during the war, but were constantly interrupted by sirens.

When he left school at fourteen, he went to work for his father's business, as did his brothers, ending up as a stock cutter. Dad, however, was a bit of a gambler and the business did not survive into the '60s, so Martin had to find other work. There was plenty of work for stock cutters, but the problem was that people were reluctant to take on boys of an age liable to be called up for National Service at any moment, and he was having to accept such lesser jobs as packing (always local), but he was at least employed. Even so, he decided to jump the gun and join up with the King's Rifle Corps (or the Green Jackets), where he trained, albeit briefly, as a rifleman.

Unfortunately, although he had passed his medical at Wanstead (another area of East London) 'A1' and been accepted for the infantry, after just eight months he was discharged as medically unfit with *hallux rigidus*, a serious foot problem, which resulted (later) in the amputation of one of his 'big' toes. Once his National Service had come to an end, it was easier to find a job as a stock cutter, and he would secure regular rises by either changing jobs or, when offered more money elsewhere, being given a rise to stop him from leaving. The ability to handle a degree of financial bluffing was to his advantage.

By 1959, and after pestering the council endlessly, the family had moved into a council flat in Woodseer Street, off Brick Lane. This larger flat, with its bathroom and hot water, seemed like sheer paradise after Felix House.

Around the same time, Martin was extending his social life from boys' clubs to such new trends as the Palais at Tottenham or Leyton, the Majestic near Tottenham Court Road (in the West End), or catching a 253 trolley bus to Stamford Hill (North London) to an early Wimpy Bar where he had his first knickerbocker glory.

In the early '60s, Martin was having treatment for his toes, which were becoming progressively worse. He attended both the London Hospital at Whitechapel and the London Jewish Hospital. More happily, Martin met Gail, a family friend, in 1963. An Essex girl but with quite a few members of her family living in Stepney, she remembers her grandfather's fish and chip shop, Benny's, in Backchurch Lane.

Their wedding in 1965 was at Great Garden Street synagogue, Greatorex Street, but his parents did not attend, as the arrangements had caused much friction – both with regard to money and with regard to which relatives should be invited. The couple moved in with Gail's dad in Westcliff-on-Sea for a few years, but moved back to his mum's around 1969 until she found them another flat via her landlord. This was another slum clearance property, in Heneage Street, where they stayed for a couple of years until being re-housed on the fifteenth floor of a tower block – Waterview House, Carr Street on the edge of Stepney Green.

Sitting in their comfortable home in Westcliff-on-Sea, with the sun shining in, they speak fondly of Carr Street. They had been stunned by the views, the warmth (after the damp they were used to) and 'would still be there today' if they hadn't had children, as you weren't 'allowed' children above the fifth floor!

# LILIAN GREENSLADE

## *Plenty to Smile About*

If anyone had a busy 1950s, then Lilian did. By 1957, she had five children under ten. The eldest, Brenda, was born in 1948, and in 1950 they were living at no. 37 Great Eastern Buildings in Quaker Street (off Brick Lane), the year that John was born (at home, in the presence of a midwife and a doctor who was learning midwifery). Her husband, known as Jack, worked for several decades at paint manufacturer Thomas Smith's on the corner of Sidney Street, a bicycle ride away.

Great Eastern Buildings offered a concrete area for local children to play in, plus a flat roof as an extra play area, and the fascination of the railway yards at the end of the street. The block had three storeys, with an outside loo shared by four families, the flat having just two rooms, one for living and cooking and one for sleeping. There was a gas stove in the living room for cooking, and there was a sink for washing, but that was the extent of mod cons.

To boost the family income as her brood grew, Lilian took in piece work for local dressmakers, doing finishing work by hand. This isn't something she enjoyed, but she regarded it as a necessity, in spite of the long hours she needed to put in to earn a decent wage.

After Anthony was born in 1951, the Greenslades asked the council for a larger place, and moved into Hughes Mansions in Vallance Road in 1952. Here they were on the top floor of a five-storey block, which, although not a new build, had three bedrooms, a separate kitchen, a bathroom with toilet, and even a dining room: bliss. There was no lift, so the pram had to be bumped up the stairs – and when a bigger pram was needed it was kept in the ground floor pram shed, with the small pram kept for the essential shunting. This bigger pram, a large maroon Swan (a gift) which could take three incumbents, had such a big chassis and wheels that not only would it not fit on the balcony that ran along the outside of the upper flats, but Lilian's small frame had a problem manoeuvring it successfully. As a result, the wheels were replaced with much smaller ones – in cream, not maroon. You might be able to spot the pram (and its occupiers) in a background scene of *A Kid for Two Farthings*, filmed locally in 1955.

This pram did sterling duty to and from the nearest market, Bethnal Green Road, where Lilian could spend her Providence cheques on clothes (there were also vouchers for the children's shoes). At weekends, it took them further afield to Shadwell Park and Victoria Park. When they were a bit older, the children enjoyed the paddling pool at 'Barmy Park' (reference to an early lunatic asylum) on the corner of Cambridge Heath Road and Green Street. This was a favourite during school holidays.

Lilian's parents lived in a terraced house in Sidney Street with her brother and his wife and son. Her mum worked as a school cleaner and her dad helped out a local builder. It was at this

*Lilian carrying Anthony at a family wedding, Limehouse Town Hall, 1951. John and Brenda are at the front.*
*(Greenslade collection)*

house that Lilian and her family watched the Coronation in 1953 – fifteen of them (including neighbours) crammed into a small room to watch a twelve-inch screen.

Soon after, Brenda started primary school – at Deal Street. The other children followed in her footsteps, including Frank (born 1954) and Paul (1957). Brenda recalls Deal Street as having dark corridors, and she remembers lining up for school dinners every day and the cod liver oil tablet that was dished out with the tepid milk at morning break. A significant teacher was Miss T., a tall, strict Australian, who used a system of phonetic signing – successfully – to help the children learn to read. Then there was Mr B., an ex RAF officer who carried his cane and liked to bring it crashing down on the nearest desk or table, and Miss B., who had obvious favourites among the children. It seems that John, who admits to being a stubborn child, was not one of her favourites, and, because he refused to talk to her, she arranged for him to see a psychiatrist at University College Hospital. As Lilian's own doctor gave his consent, they felt obliged to attend this appointment, which turned out to be completely futile, as John had no problems once he changed classes.

Back at home, Lilian was still busy. She used a boiler to wash the clothes and nappies, hanging them up to dry on a line in the kitchen, and she could be seen scrubbing the stairs of the flats every week, even when pregnant, it being an unspoken 'duty', with all the tenants taking a turn. Apart from shopping for her main rations in Bethnal Green Road, she would also frequent Sadie's, a little shop at the bottom of the flats, with mainly Jewish customers.

As for milk, that was delivered by Les, the United Dairies' milkman. Coal was delivered in 5cwt bags, which had to be carried up the stairs. Lilian made a point of counting the bags, which were carried through the kitchen and kept in the kitchen cupboard.

The annual holiday was hop-picking in Kent, which could also include scrumping for apples. There was also the occasional day trip by train to Southend-on-Sea, especially on the day that the seafront illuminations were switched on, which did mean that the children were extra tired coming home. Later, they bought themselves a tent on the 'never never' and took it to a field in Somerset. Additionally, the Dean Swift pub (in Deancross Street) would arrange an annual outing by charabanc for the local children to a West End pantomime (usually at the London Palladium). This was paid for by contributions from customers over the year, and it was granddad who paid every week for the Greenslade children.

At Christmas, the children did receive at least one worthwhile present each, apart from small extras such as sweets. Brenda's all-time favourite was an iron and ironing board (not something she'd appreciate now), while Frankie's was a set of bricklaying materials used by all the children to build houses, using paste and a trowel, which could be knocked down and rebuilt again in a different form. There was also a reproduction of an old-fashioned stagecoach one year – pedal powered. Everyone had an annual (*Bunty, Dandy, Beano* etc.) which were paid for in instalments at the local newsagents in Vallance Road. Their television was bought at Wally for Wireless in Whitechapel Road, and furniture was bought at Jay's, which involved regular trips to the first floor to pay the instalments.

All the children went to Saturday morning pictures at the ABC in Mile End Road, and attended Sunday School at the Good Shepherd Mission in Three Colts Lane (Bethnal Green). As for Lilian, she managed an evening out once a year – on Christmas Eve – when neighbours

*'Barmy' Park. From left to right: Frank, Paul, John, Brenda, Anthony. (Greenslade collection)*

*Lilian, her mother and Brenda hop-picking in Kent. (Greenslade collection)*

*John (left) next to Brenda with charabanc taking them to London Palladium. (Greenslade collection)*

looked after the children so she and her husband could go out for a drink at The George in Vallance Road. There was one memorable beano arranged by the dressmaking factory she worked for in the '50s when Paul was just three months old, meaning her husband rather disapproved. This was a day out for the girls in Brighton, when she wore a dress made for her by her 'forelady' – memorable partly because somebody stole the petrol from the coach at some point, making the return journey much lengthier than planned.

Once all five children were born, the Greenslades applied again for a bigger dwelling, and moved in December 1962 to Dagobert House in Smithy Street. This was a brand new maisonette on the ground floor with four bedrooms. The only minor flaws on moving in were the weather – a cold, snowy, wet winter which meant they didn't see the grass until April – and the building going on around them which meant mud everywhere for months on end. Anthony ended up at the Jewish hospital (the nearest hospital with a Casualty Department) when he trapped his fingers in a part-built construction on the site – but the 'hot needle' he was subjected to certainly taught him a lesson.

During the 1960s, the children were growing up and progressing to secondary education. Brenda went to Robert Montefiore School, and the boys went to Dempsey Street School, which was split during this period into Stepney Green School in Ben Jonson Road (for the boys) with the girls sent to Tower Hamlet School in Richard Street, off Commercial Road. Uniforms were an expensive outgoing for the Greenslades. When Mr Rhodes Boyson (later an MP and a Sir) took over as head of Robert Montefiore, he changed the uniform from navy to dark green and introduced a summer and winter uniform, involving a substantial extra outlay. At Dempsey Street, the boys had to buy everything at Eden's in Ben Jonson Road. Not only a black blazer with the school badge, but a tie in the house colours, woodwork aprons, rugby and football kit with special socks to match and even cardigans with the school emblem. At least Lilian could re-sew the blazer pocket complete with logo onto a market outfit as the years progressed, which did save some money.

To boost their spending power, John and Anthony had newspaper rounds, earning enough to buy bicycles. The Krays were on their round (in Vallance Road), although it was usually Violet, the mother, that they would come into contact with. It seems the bills never got paid, but they were good tippers at Christmas. John recalls the road being blocked off when Ginger Marks disappeared in 1965 after being shot, the only time the papers didn't get delivered.

At school, the boys were introduced to a number of sports. John represented Stepney Green School in rugby and cross country, Frankie did horse-riding, Paul basketball, and in the last year they were introduced to a broader range, including golf and sailing.

Away from school, Lilian encouraged the children to join local clubs, but, again, they seemed to favour anything with a uniform: scouts at Roland House in Stepney Green for all four boys and the Girls' Life Brigade for Brenda. Once they were teenagers, they discovered Toynbee Hall in Commercial Street. Brenda liked the country dancing on Saturday mornings, and John and Anthony liked the drama group which put on such productions as *Treasure Island* and *Androcles and the Lion*, John favouring back-stage work. The drama group on Friday evenings and Saturday mornings (for teenagers) was funded by the ILEA and used professional directors for the plays, three or four every year.

Brenda left school in 1964 and went to work as a nursery nurse in Underwood Road at Mary Hughes' day nursery. In her spare time, she liked the live bands at the Prospect of Whitby

*Lilian (in the check dress) on a working girls' outing. (Greenslade collection)*

*John's ID, 1966. (Greenslade collection)*

on Friday evenings, and also ventured out to the Ilford Palais (Sundays) and the Tottenham Royal (Saturdays). John left school two years later and worked as an apprentice pattern-maker at Matchbox Toys in Hackney, and Anthony also left school before the end of the '60s, serving as an apprentice engineer in Farringdon near the City of London.

The year 1967 was a memorable year – Lilian and her husband got their first car, a blue second-hand Ford Poplar. Jack Greenslade had to take his test despite having passed it once before in the army, because the licence had expired – it had cost money to renew it, money they hadn't had. The car broke down regularly, but, generally, was a useful addition to the family. It was also the year that John travelled to America to the Scouts World Jamboree (he was a scout until he was twenty) – and the year he met his wife-to-be, Irene, at the Toynbee Hall drama group.

Lilian's family were growing up and leaving home – but it seems she did a very good job.

# THE HALLIDAYS

## *Working Nine to Five*

Now living in Leigh-on-Sea, Jean and Arthur Halliday grew up in Stepney, living in Jamaica Street until the late 1950s. This home was a Victorian terrace, with a backyard and outside toilet, a tin bath which was used in the kitchen, and a coal-cellar. It was big enough for them to be able to have a bedroom each, their older sister and brother having married and moved out by the '50s. The presence of a piano – and of a dog – made the house a home, as did their mother's excellent cooking.

At the start of the '50s, Jean was a teenager attending Raines Foundation School in Arbour Square, but she left before 'O' levels to get out into the world of work. The uniform at Raines was a navy blue gymslip and pale blue blouse, with summer dresses of blue and white cotton, the uniform made up by an outfitter's at Gardiner's Corner, on the edge of the City. The school had a choir which would later give concerts in such locations as The People's Palace, and it also had its own magazine, *The Rainian*.

Amongst the teachers, Jean recalls the head, Miss Haugh, who strode around in her mortar board and gown, and Mrs Weingarten, the History teacher, whose husband was a classical pianist and gave occasional recitals at the school. On such occasions, the large glass doors which separated the girls and the boys at Raines were opened up, but this was the only time the genders mixed. Every week a coach-load of girls were taken to Fairlop for hockey practice, but Jean's abiding memory of school is of the excessive homework.

During the Coronation, older brother Harry brought over a black-and-white television, which they were pretty much glued to all day. But they did take part in the local street party, which was on quite a grand scale, with small side stages where local talent could show off their dancing and variety skills. Other local residents even dragged their pianos into the street.

Jean's first job was in the classified advertising department of WH Smith's in The Strand, which involved a daily tube journey from Stepney Green station, at a time when you could actually get a seat. She stayed there through the '50s and had similar office jobs during the '60s. When work was over, a favourite venue was the London Palladium, again only a tube ride away, where she saw such names as Howard Keel, Eddie Fisher and Debbie Reynolds. Her friends were mainly her work colleagues, as most school friends had stayed on at Raines. Window shopping was another favourite occupation, mainly in the West End, but the Hallidays also favoured the local Wickham's in Mile End Road, the Harrods of Stepney, for larger purchases such as curtains and bedding – the store assistants utilised tubes on overhead wires for the cash payments, and change came back the same way.

Their mum was another stay-at-home mum, and dad, Harry, worked at the Shipping Federation in Mansell Street, Aldgate. Harry was a first officer in the merchant navy, and, after

*Raines Foundation building, now a college, 2009. (Dee Gordon)*

*Arbour Square, 2009. (Dee Gordon)*

*Jean and relatives in Dempsey Street,
1950s. (Halliday collection)*

*Ocean Estate, 2009. (Dee Gordon)*

the war, worked – in full uniform – at repatriating naval staff. He also did hands-on teaching – from ratings to officers – at sea schools in locations such as the Vindicatrix in East India Docks, which involved boating drills, naval skills, and the ubiquitous knots.

In 1957, the family moved to Levant House, a high-rise on a new estate – the Ocean Estate in Mile End Road. Although they had no central heating, the flats were easier to maintain than their old house, with a bathroom. Their mother, Elsie, took pride in the outside as well as the inside of her domain, taking her turn to clean the stairs to the first floor where they lived. The family never had a car, but they did have one of the first telephones in the area.

As a family, they would spend occasional evenings at the local Bricklayers' Arms in Hannibal Road, known locally as Jim Meads', the owner's name. But it wasn't unusual to go to the cinema several times in one week, and Jean and Arthur were spoilt for choice – although they rarely went together (Arthur is nearly ten years older than Jean). They could choose from the Mile End Odeon, the ABC, the Ben Hur in Watney Street, the Troxy in Commercial Road, or the Foresters in Cambridge Heath Road, and were happy to queue literally for hours to see something featuring a favourite star. There was also an occasional outing to the People's Palace in Mile End Road, which staged musicals, a family favourite. Holidays were usually taken at Great Yarmouth, with day trips to Southend-on-Sea.

Arthur also spent the 1950s and '60s working, but as a case-maker. He had followed in his older brother's footsteps into the profession, and always worked within walking distance

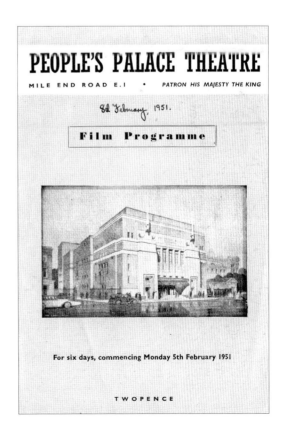

*People's Palace programme, 1951. (Dee Gordon collection)*

for a variety of local packing-case makers, never being out of work. He also took on all the decorating at home, doing this kind of work for others in his spare time for extra cash. One of his bosses had a boat moored at Rainham, Essex, and he would even do some maintenance work on that.

At home, he wasn't keen on using the portable metal bath in the kitchen, with its potential lack of privacy, and instead frequented the Municipal Baths near Stepney Green station. These had individual cubicles, with men and women kept completely separate, and an assistant pacing up and down outside. If you needed more towels, soap, bath crystals, or water – all at extra cost – you would simply yell out and he would find you, serve you, and expect a tip in return. He'd expect an even bigger tip if he put a towel down on the cold tiled floor for you to tread on when you got out.

When he wasn't working – or at the cinema – Arthur spent some time in the local pubs, but on Sundays preferred to go fishing in the nearby Thames with members of a fishing club. There would be time at the weekend to pop in to Kelly's in Mile End Road for pie and mash, buy a new Bing Crosby record for his radiogram, or visit one of the Jewish tailors in Mile End Road or Commercial Road to have a new suit made.

The siblings have fond memories of Christmases in Stepney. Their parents had quite a big family who were all welcome, and would be happy to sleep on the floor or in any available chair. Beer was bought in by the barrel, and there were often two turkeys, one bought and one given to their father as a Christmas gift. Their mother didn't just bake one Christmas cake and one Christmas pudding, but a number of each, to cater for visitors. On Christmas morning, a trader with a barrow of shell-fish was a regular sight in the '50s, and Jean would be sent out in her new Christmas slippers with an apron over her new Christmas dress to buy supplies for Christmas 'tea'.

# PAM JENKIN

*Strict – But Fair*

Before 1950, Pam was living with her parents on the top floor of a terraced house in Walden Street (behind London Hospital), with her grandparents downstairs. Although the space was confined, her parents still put aside one room to store the furniture they were collecting for their own home which they moved into at the start of the '50s – in Blount House, off Stepney High Street, the area now known as Limehouse.

David, Florence and their daughter ended up on the top floor, the fourth, with urban views. Although the block of flats may not have been brand new, it was of course a luxury for Pam to have her own bedroom and to have a bathroom and inside loo. She did not have her own bedroom for long, however, as her sister Linda was born in 1950 at the small maternity hospital in Commercial Street – known locally, even by the bus conductors, as The Stork Club. While her mother was in hospital (for the requisite week) and her dad was working as a lorry driver, Pam stayed with her aunt and uncle in Hackney.

One story shows that having a new sister around was not all roses, because Pam's favourite china doll, bought for her by her aunt and uncle when she was three, was smashed when Linda dropped it on the doorstep. Up till then, her favourite presents at Christmas had been baby clothes for her doll, so this was a sad day.

An early memory of her first school in Caley Street is of the school hall, which the children had to cross if summoned to see the headmistress, Mrs McHarrie. The summons need not be for a reprimand; it could be to demonstrate your reading skills, for which – if satisfactory – you received a jelly baby. The sound of Pam's shoes crossing the hall and climbing the staircase to the head's office is still clear in her memory. The hall was also the place for an annual celebration of Empire Day in the '50s – on the 24 May – when children turned up at school in their brownie or cub uniform.

School, however, does not generally hold fond memories for Pam. She was a shy child, someone who didn't speak up for herself. This meant that her form teacher grew somewhat frustrated by her unwillingness to raise her hand when she knew an answer, and complained to her mother. She was also punished for confusing the spelling of 'their' and 'there' with a ruler across the knuckles and 100 lines – but it worked, because she didn't confuse them any longer. There was also the embarrassment of having to stand (in front of your classmates) if you scored less than six out of ten in a mental arithmetic test, or, if you scored less than four, standing on the chair, emphasising your lack of prowess.

After school was far more pleasant. There were a lot of children in the surrounding flats and cottages, and they played outside in the traffic-free grounds – rounders, skipping, tin tan tommy (a bit like hide-and-seek, where you had to hide while the person that was 'it' caught a tin can

*Pam's sister Linda at play.*
*(Pam Jenkin collection)*

*Pam (right) and Linda on a*
*bombsite. (Pam Jenkin collection)*

*Pam (left) and Linda at 'Old*
*Road Park'. (Pam Jenkin*
*collection)*

*Pam's sister Sandra (left) at Caley Street School. (Pam Jenkin collection)*

that had been thrown) and ball games. Some had roller skates which Pam remembers borrowing, and she also recalls a scooter which you propelled with one foot and which took you at some speed along the balconies. A favoured occupation was putting on 'shows' on the stairs of the flats for other children, charging a halfpenny for them to watch, which was spent on sweets (for the audience). Although shy, Pam rather enjoyed 'directing' the singing and dancing children, and she also enjoyed taking others to the local park known as Old Road Park (next to St Dunstan's Church) or for a picnic on the adjacent hump of grassland known as Dead Man's Belly.

When Pam ventured on one occasion (c. 1953) a little further afield, to Shadwell Park, she knew she had to be home by 9 p.m. but didn't have a watch. Obviously worried about being late home, she had to leave her friends and walk home alone, a daunting experience for someone without a sense of direction, and she didn't make it in time. As a result, although she was very upset by the experience, her cross mother insisted she go straight to bed without anything to eat. However, her dad seemingly felt a bit sorry for his daughter so he sneaked her in some bread and jam.

There was obviously a community spirit in the area in the '50s. There were organised coach trips – one to a circus at Earls Court. When there were local disasters, such as when a boy drowned while fishing on the canal, everyone rallied round to comfort the grieving family.

Pam was not a great joiner-inner. She did try the Brownies, but only for a few visits, and she also did go one Sunday with her sister to a local church – but was petrified at being confronted with a nun at the entrance and went straight home again.

The Jenkins invested in their first television after the Coronation. They had watched the ceremony on a nine-inch set belonging to a friend of Pam's father, and he had been so impressed that he went out and bought a Pam Pye – partly because of the name.

Family was – and is – very important to Pam. Her aunt and uncle from Hackney came over every Saturday evening, usually joined by her grandparents from Walden Street (who also came over during the week to use the bath). Most Monday evenings, she and her parents (as soon as dad had arrived home from work) would visit the Troxy or the Odeon. This continued for a while when Linda came along, but Linda's crying stopped the family visiting, so Pam went with her dad until schoolwork left her so tired that dad would have to carry her home. Her mum was always around, as David did not approve of his wife working.

An occasion when Florence wasn't around, of course, was when another daughter, Sandra, came along in 1955. By now, Pam had started secondary school and, coincidentally, there had been a lot of talk at the school about a film the fourth years had seen on the subject of pregnancy and birth. As a result of the gossip, all the younger pupils were shown this film – which came as a bit of a shock to Pam, because Florence had told her that her large tummy was due to excess milk!

Pam's secondary education was at Sir Martin Frobisher in Halley Street, where her teacher, Mr Lasota, a Polish immigrant who had lost all his family in the war and had fought against the Germans, made quite an impression. He is certainly one of the few she remembers with any fondness, even though he, too, would use the cane when he felt it necessary. After several months here, Pam's mother was called in to discuss the idea of Pam going to a Polytechnic in Shoreditch, but neither were keen, so Pam stayed put.

As for holidays, these were always shared with aunt, uncle, and cousins, the whole family cramming into a hired car and ending up in a caravan or chalet in Devon, Cornwall, or Somerset, which they used as a base for local exploration. Pam's father, incidentally, learnt to drive when in the army during the war, and therefore avoided the civilian driving test. For these holidays, the family saved all year round in a loan club, and the children also saved with a Christmas Club. Bank holiday treats were outings to Essex resorts – Clacton, Canvey, Walton and Epping Forest.

After school, as a teenager, Pam wasn't allowed to visit the youth clubs, though school dances were 'allowed'. Occasionally she would take some of the local children to the Ben Hur cinema (known locally as the Bug Hole), but she didn't favour the Troxy as it was too noisy and too big. She did spend a few evenings at classes in office procedures, but these didn't last, as they spent two weeks learning how to use a paper clip. For a girl who had been using a typewriter at home (bought by her uncle when she was thirteen), this was not too stimulating.

In 1959, Pam left school (at fifteen). The school had a careers officer who had taken the pupils to visit a number of factories that made plastic and clay products. Although Pam liked the idea of working in an office, she had been told there 'was not a hope in hell'. However, her mother asked around to see if there were any junior opportunities and came up with a job in Old Broad Street, a bus ride from Stepney East. Pam started work – with N.W. Spratt, a chartering/shipping agency – before officially leaving school, returning only to finish the term.

With her first week's salary, she bought her mother a dressing gown (because she was the only one in the family without one), her dad forty cigarettes, and her sisters big bags of sweets. As a result, she had to borrow money from her mum to get to work the second week. Most of her money from then on went on clothes, and she was working close to Petticoat Lane, an ideal place to spend lunch hours. After a year at Spratt's, they were taken over, which involved a move to nearby Houndsditch, where they became part of Mitchell Cotts. An interesting

*Pam's bridesmaids, including Linda (centre) and Sandra on her right. (Pam Jenkin collection)*

*Pam on her wedding day. (Pam Jenkin collection)*

memory of working in the City is of the very thick fogs that would occasionally descend. Pam recalls walking from the City to her nan's home in Walden Street, where she had to feel the walls to find her way. Although her father gave her a lift back to Blount House, the fog was so bad that her Uncle Ron walked in front of the car with a torch to see them home.

Even now, Pam was still happy for her social life to revolve around family – although her father would occasionally take her and her girl-friends (from school days), Barbara and Veronica, to the Ilford Palais. The girls took turns to stay over at each other's houses, three of them sharing a single bed. They would help each other with their '60s bouffant hairdos the next morning. Similarly, at Christmas, family would arrive *en masse* and share beds quite happily for a day or two.

It's not too surprising then that she met her husband, Barry, at work. He was one of the lads who liked to go dancing at the Lyceum in the Strand at lunchtime, but Pam, predictably, was banned from this particular activity. Incidentally, she seems to hold no resentment for her strict upbringing, far from it.

Her first boyfriend from Mitchell Cotts had taken her to see Adam Faith, Billy Fury (her favourite) and bought her expensive gifts such as Chanel No. 5. But Barry, her preference, was content with an occasional cinema trip – after all, they could see each other all day every day at work ... He worked in the Insurance Department, and was an Essex boy whose mother seems to have thought he could do better than an 'East End girl'.

At work, Pam progressed to working in the telex department, a job which she enjoyed, but which meant working late hours, which did not suit her once she married. Their wedding was at St Dunstan's in November 1965, with a live band at their reception at Collett Hall, the numbers considerably boosted when Barry invited his football team, the Progress Rovers.

As the Jenkins moved to a flat in Stratford after their marriage, their Stepney story ends here. They have since returned to Barry's Essex roots, where he no longer has to struggle to translate the Cockney rhyming slang Pam's family favoured.

# THE KEEPERS

## *Singing and Dancing*

At the beginning of the '50s, Henrietta (known as Joan) and Joseph Keeper were living with baby Lesley in Cranberry Street, off Vallance Road. This was a cul-de-sac and they were at the end, the smallest house in the street, near to the freight train depot. Outside was a cobblestone slope leading up through big iron gates into the goods yard, with lorries in and out all day. Opposite lived the Mitchells (Ada, Johnny, and two daughters Melody and Georgina), with the Liverpool Street main line running behind them. Ada worked her whole life at the Charrington's Brewery.

The Keepers lived at number 14b and Joseph's mother (one of twenty-one children) lived at number 19. The beautiful garden at 19 was complimented (in spite of the rabbit hutches) by no less than the Queen Mother who was judging a garden competition, one entry being the garden next door. It seems that the Queen Mother mentioned that grandma's garden would have made a better entry! Granny Keeper is remembered for her discipline, but also for her work ethic – she did all her washing by hand using a washboard with Sunlight Soap and ICI soaking crystals, and a mangle.

Until the old lady living at 14b died, they had all lived at 19. It had taken a big lorry to remove all this old lady's belongings – including hoards of newspapers and bottles – which were stacked in bags up to the ceilings. Luckily, Joseph had always been good at DIY and the house was quickly re-vamped.

Granddad had a coal delivery business, with stables nearby in Hemming Street, and often brought the horse and cart home at mealtimes. When the horse (a shire, called Nigger) was outside the house, he deposited plenty of manure, very handy for the garden, and a contribution to the splendid display of roses. The cart – more of an open-top lorry – was well known in the area with its prominent sign 'Keeper's Coals'.

Joseph was also employed in the '50s in his father's business. They delivered sacks of coal in many local areas including Hackney and Bow, and, when the sacks were damaged, Joseph would repair them with tar, a messy but essential and effective job. He had other skills, making wooden musical boxes in such detailed shapes as a heart or a piano, and larger items such as a padded and sectioned needlework box, which Lesley still uses. Later on, he taught Lesley carpentry and DIY skills.

Another two girls – Linda and Lorraine – were born to the Keepers in the '50s at Mile End Hospital, Bancroft Road. While the girls were very young, Joan did homework for a tassel factory, hand sewing dozens of them for some extra money. The family just managed to run a car, and had a black-and-white television in time for the Coronation. It was their grandma

*Jim Keeper (Joe's brother) at the stables in Selby Street, 1950s. (Lesley Keeper collection)*

*Joan Keeper in Bartman's machine room, New Road, 1960s. (Lesley Keeper collection)*

who had the first television in the street, however, a cumbersome Baird, which Lesley always thought was called a Bear.

As a young girl in the '50s, Lesley regarded the local bomb-sites as playgrounds. You could build a bonfire on one and bake potatoes, or you could lay a board down (supplied by a local dad) and practice tap dancing. As she got older, she progressed to earning the princely sum of 10s clearing caterpillars from her grandparents' garden.

Local children were fond of watching – through the iron gates – the men in the goods yard loading parcels onto the trucks, workers with brown overalls and either a pen or cigarette behind their ears. Linda, born in the mid-'50s, remembers the sound of the trucks shunting during the night, and found it comforting throughout her childhood. When leaving Vallance Road, you had to wait for a railwayman in full uniform with cap, gold stripes down the side of his trousers, waistcoat and fob watch, to give you clearance to pass over the tracks – complete with whistle and red flag. There was the potential bonus of spotting either the rag-and-bone man, the knife-sharpener (who also sharpened scissors), or the Corona (drinks) man. Linda also remembers the Corporation Cleansing Department who left every drain in the street with strong smelling pink powder that could 'knock your head back'.

Lesley's first school was Hague Street Primary in E2. Here, the forward-thinking Mr Golding taught his class French in their final year. She didn't like milk, so when the free school bottles were handed round, she secretly swapped her full one with a friend's empty one because such 'faddiness' would not have been tolerated. The lucky friend was usually Patsy Adams, but could have been Evelyn, Janice, or another Patsy. When Lesley moved on to Robert Montefiore Secondary School in Vallance Road, the (Welsh) headmaster at the time was Rhodes Boyson, before his days as an MP.

As for Joan, she was always looking for opportunities to sing, a life-long passion. She had learned to harmonise with her own father. During the '50s, she sang with the McGill Five for a while, one of many feathers in her cap.

In January 1959, the growing family moved to a flat in Cambridge Heath Road, above a row of shops. Joseph went with the removal van and Linda, Joan and Lesley walked, pushing the Silver Cross pram filled with kettles, pots, pans and homewares with one-year-old Lorraine perched on top. The day they moved in, Linda remembers peering through the curtains to watch the men removing the old trolleybus overhead wires. No more tin bath, two toilets, and a balcony on which Joseph could grow geraniums.

Because of the location, it was planned that Lesley should move to Morpeth Secondary Modern (E2), but she wanted to stay with her friends and continued at Robert Montefiore in spite of the long walk. She still has part of her navy school uniform which included a beret and striped tie.

At this school, she acquired a taste for netball, although smaller than the rest of the team, but did have one bad experience when one of the boys who was tormenting her during a practice session butted her on the nose – which was later revealed to have been broken. School dinners here catered for the growing Jewish population, and separate kosher and non-kosher meals were served. The children formed two separate queues, taking turns as to which queue went first, and there would be such distinctions as custard made with water rather than milk for the Jewish students.

One of Lesley's friends at school was the caretaker's daughter, Linda. The caretaker lived on the premises, with one door to the playground and one to the street, and occasionally Lesley

*The Coronation celebrations in Hemming Street, 1953. Lesley is in the front row, one from the right with blazer and white shoes. (Lesley Keeper collection)*

and Linda would use this as an escape from lessons. However, Linda's family kept an Alsatian dog, which, although generally friendly when the two girls were together, did not take kindly to Lesley trying to 'bunk off' alone on one occasion, and attacked her with some venom. Only her thick winter clothing kept her from serious injury.

Something else Lesley recalls from her teens was the tendency for so many of her peers to smoke in the school toilets. The smokers would extend the life of their cigarettes by pushing a hairgrip into the base so that the stub could be smoked down to the very, very bottom. Another economy was the use of the small, oddly-shaped, 3*d* bits to serve as substitute when, for stocking wearers, the suspender notch broke.

During the early '60s, when such dances as 'The Locomotion' were fashionable with the teenage population, Lesley and her chums would practice in the school corridors at playtime. The school itself would put on regular dances for pupils throughout the year. At least one pupil went further than dancing at the school hops and went on to dance and sing on stage (in, for example, *Cats* and *Oliver!*) and television.

Linda and Lorraine both attended Cephas Street Infants before moving on to John Scurr Primary, and then Morpeth Secondary in Bethnal Green. It was at Cephas that Linda was taught to read by Miss Hewitt, the headmistress, courtesy of the Janet and John books. At secondary school, she was in Wentworth House (green), while Lorraine, several years younger, was in Gresham (yellow), and it seemed that Wentworth always lagged behind top-dogs

*Cranberry Street bombsite. Linda Keeper is one from the right. (Lesley Keeper collection)*

*Lesley Keeper with her granddad Jim in Petticoat Lane, c. 1955. (Lesley Keeper collection)*

*Robert Montefiore Secondary School Netball Team (third year), 1961. Lesley is on the right at the front (with a black eye). (Lesley Keeper collection)*

*Joan Keeper at the Well and Bucket, 1960s. (Lesley Keeper collection)*

Gresham. The House Mistress of Ridley (red) was the very strict Mrs Thompson, who was also head of History, a subject Linda enjoyed.

Linda enjoyed netball at primary school, and dance classes from an early age at Christine Hawkes School of Dancing in Oxford House, Bethnal Green. She was a pupil there for five years, until discovering boys at the age of thirteen towards the end of the '60s, just two exams away from becoming a tap-dancing teacher. The dancing school put on shows, mainly locally, for which Linda won plenty of certificates and trophies, with Joan often the compère and singer because of her outstanding singing voice. Linda won a junior dance championship in the National Dance Category by doing a Swedish National Dance in full costume.

In 1964, Lesley, the oldest daughter, left school after staying on for six months to study shorthand and typing. For her first job, she visited an employment agency in Aldgate, and started the following Monday in the offices of tailors Ellis and Goldstein. A numerate employee, she took on responsibility for wages and clocking in machines, the only person in the department who did not need a calculator. After about a year, she moved on to a wholesale chemist's in Petticoat Lane, taking orders over the telephone, but her cockney accent did not seem to go down too well with the Jewish brothers who owned the company – and she was fired. Her friend, Jennifer, did manage to put on a 'posh' voice while at work, promptly changing back at the end of the day. It seems that the brothers regretted their decision, because, after Lesley got a job at Bethnal Green Hospital also doing wages, they asked her to go back: she didn't.

As a teenager, Lesley favoured the Bruce Club at St Hilda's in the East on the Boundary Estate near Shoreditch – a youth club patronised by the Kray twins – which offered a variety of activities including piano and table tennis. Once she was working, she would get the bus to such dance halls as the Tottenham Royal in North London, a 'Mod' venue – and soon learned that boys would only give her a lift home if she said she lived in 'Tower Hamlets' rather than in 'Stepney'. If she did have to walk, she would take off her white stilettos and go barefoot as it was much easier. There was a late-night drinking club in a converted house in Victoria Park Road, which only allowed couples, and there was a live music venue in Mare Street (Hackney) where Lesley remembers seeing The Who and collecting autographs from Roger Daltrey and Keith Moon.

She also indulged in a Friday visit to the hairdresser for a bouffant beehive, leaving it pretty much untouched all week apart from a comb-out – again at the hairdresser's – midweek. For her clothes, Lesley was a fan of the Beatles-style suits that she would have made up in mohair at a tailor's in Brady Street.

It was around this time that mum, Joan, was working at Anchor Insurance in the Claims Department, so Lesley would take her two sisters to school, and take them to the park in the holidays etc.

In 1966, Lesley married Peter, a distant relative she had known since schooldays. They were wed at St Peter's Church in Bethnal Green, with a reception in the Arabian Arms on the corner of Cambridge Heath Road and Bishop's Way (now Metropolis, a strip club!). Peter, who worked for Truman's Brewery locally, was a DJ at this pub, and one of the singers was famous locally as Diamond Lil.

At the start of their marriage, they lived with Peter's sister in Patriot Square (near Roberta Taylor, now an actress and author) and then with his mum at Canrobert Street (both in Bethnal Green) until after their children were born. Terrie was born in London Hospital, promptly followed by Tracy – the latter's birth being a tad premature. Lesley had been on a train journey to Canvey Island to be witness at a friend's wedding, but had labour pains before the wedding, meaning that Tracy was born in Rochford Hospital, Southend. Peter took Terrie to the wedding, and the newlyweds had to find another witness in a bit of a hurry.

By the end of the '60s, the young family were living back with Peter's sister, adding to her own brood of five. Luckily, the house was big enough for them all. The oldest of Lesley's nieces looked after the babies while Lesley worked part-time for Alison's the bakers (known for their rather revolutionary low calorie rolls).

As for Joan – who adopted the name at her first job when she felt Henrietta sounded 'too posh' – she was able to pursue her love of singing. She sang around the local pubs for her supper, or in competitions. One memorable competition was at the Well and Bucket (Bethnal Green) when she won a tea-set; she was 'persuaded' to swap this for a satchel, which she still has – although, decades later, she still regrets the loss of that tea-set.

# THE KUYPERS

## *Still Living the East End Life*

Quite a few Kuypers lived in Perth Street, Stepney, in the 1950s and 1960s. Albert, married to Alice since 1949, lived there thanks to a tip-off from his parents who also lived in the street, as did his brothers. The young couple met when working at Jules Duval (wines) in Bermondsey, having first 'clapped eyes' on each other (to quote Albert) around the bottle washing machine. Albert learned a variety of skills here from ordering through to labelling, bottling, binning, stacking and even brewing.

Alice gave up work when their first daughter, Pauline, was born. Their home was a one-bedroom terrace with brick-built wash-house or scullery, the terrace since replaced with flats. This stayed their home following the premature birth of another daughter, Jacqueline, but, because Jacqueline was born blind and disabled, she, sadly, spent most of her time at the Sunshine Home in Swanley, Kent. Albert actually offered to donate an eye, hoping to help Jacqueline, but medical science had not progressed that far.

The family did get together at weekends, and another daughter, Tracy, was born in 1961, making their home very cosy indeed. Tracy, incidentally, was born in Mile End (or Bancroft) Hospital at a time when Princess Marina was visiting the maternity ward, so she had a right royal welcome into the world. Alice had a large perambulator for her babies, too large to get into their small hall, so it was kept at a brother-in-law's. She pushed the pram regularly over Tower Bridge to visit her own family in Deptford – quite a feat in today's terms.

Pauline's first school was Marion Richardson (or Senrab Street) School, which had a separate playground for the very young ones. In the afternoons, they were provided with camp beds and told, firmly, to shut their eyes, reinforced by a teacher walking up and down. Her next school was Dempsey Street (long gone) Secondary, with its navy blue uniform, where she enjoyed the netball and the running. She represented her school at the latter in competitions at Eton Manor (soon to be used for the Paralympics 2012), winning certificates for which she was justifiably proud. She was also quite good at Pitman's shorthand, taught by Mrs Flenner (*sic*) who also taught typing.

As a young girl, Pauline's favourite doll was a black-skinned model which she called Winifred after the singer Winifred Atwell. Her favourite present on a special occasion such as Christmas was a pair of plastic high heels, although these had a very short life in practical terms. As for her favourite past-time, this was having tea parties with her dolls, using real mini loaves of Hovis. A few years later, and she was into flared skirts and drawing a line up the back of her leg to imitate stocking seams. For a thirteenth birthday in the '60s, her present was a Dansette record player.

Family Sundays at this time were spent at home, especially as Alice took on cooking the Sunday lunch for Albert's two brothers, for anyone else who cared to drop in, and for the elderly lady next door who had meals-on-wheels the rest of the week. When this lady, Bobby, moved to a home in Senrab Street, Albert would continue to take her Sunday lunch to her – on a tray. In the evening, Father Sawell from nearby St Dunstan's came to them – he would settle down for a cup of tea, and was befriended by the family cat, Blackie, who sat on his lap. On Thursdays, pay-day, everyone had a treat from Jacob's in Commercial Road – usually a chocolate flake or nut brittle.

The family had their first 'proper' holiday in 1961 with friends of Alice's – in Jersey. This was quite an adventure for them all, as previous 'holidays' were mainly fruit-picking in Kent, although Albert always seemed to get a heat rash – proving, if nothing else, that summers were actually sunny.

At Christmas time, 'Uncle Dick' nearly always managed to get a big turkey from the meat market, so big that it could just about be squeezed into their small oven – or, if not a turkey, then it would be an extra large box of fruit from the fruit market. He brought friends home from the pub for Christmas dinner, and they would all happily indulge young Pauline with their spare cash. New Year would be marked by the loud singing in the street of Bobby next door, who had a loud rattle to accompany her rendition of 'Auld Lang Syne'.

When Pauline left school in 1964, she worked in Jewry Street (in the City) for an insurance company doing schedules and Lloyd's slips. By now, she was a Mod, frequenting the Blind Beggar and the Green Gate (the latter at Bethnal Green) with friends from work, although

*Mile End Hospital, 2009. (Dee Gordon)*

*St Dunstan's Church, 2009.*
*(Dee Gordon)*

her parents did not exactly approve as they were not drinkers (in spite of their wine trade background). On Sundays, she would go to a dance hall in Stratford with other Mods. It seems that local Mods would pose on their scooters up and down Commercial Road. Her musical taste ran to The Beatles (she saw them live in London), Cilla Black and the Foremost.

For her Mod clothes, Pauline shopped in local markets and on Friday lunchtime in Petticoat Lane. This was also the place where she would buy hair lacquer decanted into a squirty bottle which always seemed to leak, very stickily, but served the purpose, even though it didn't do your hair much good.

At this time, Tracy was one of the juniors at Redman's Road School in Ashfield Street, so her memories of the '60s are necessarily limited. As far as the school is concerned, however, it seems that the head, Miss Storey, lent her books to read at home, and Mrs Whitehorn was always ready with a plaster (and a cuddle) when required.

Tracy also recalls the coal cupboard under the stairs in Perth Street and the coalman who delivered the coal, raising plenty of dust, but with a lovely smell! She and Pauline now live in different parts of Essex, but have fond memories of their childhood home where the door was always open and everyone knew everyone else in the street. Their parents remain ensconced in the heart of Stepney.

# MARY PALLICAROS

## *Education, Education, Education*

Although her family are originally from Cyprus, Mary, her parents and one of her half-brothers spent the 1950s, '60s, and beyond in Stepney. Gregory and Andriana Pallicaros were the proud proprietors of the Classic Restaurant in Mile End Road (opposite Stepney Green tube station) – Gregory having bought a half share in 1950. The restaurant – which had fifteen tables on two levels – was a busy venue, serving traditional English food. Its clientele was split between local residents, the local Roland House scouts, and students from Queen Mary College nearby.

As a great believer in education, Mary's father was happy to give the students credit, and he took a personal interest in his customers, worrying whether they were eating properly when he was closed. This wasn't very often, however, as the Classic was open seven days per week until 8 p.m., even on Christmas Eve. The front of the restaurant had a few tables for the snackers, but rear tables – with tablecloths – were just as busy, and Gregory was happy to buy out his partner around 1957.

Thereafter, he had to get up early every morning to go to Smithfield for his meat (fish was hardly used because of the lingering smell), and would buy fruit from the local market in Whitechapel, although potatoes and some vegetables were delivered from Covent Garden.

The Pallicaros family lived above the shop in a two-storey flat with four bedrooms, and a large room big enough to accommodate extended family members for Christmas dinner – twenty to thirty people. There was no bathroom, of course, but the public baths were literally across the road.

As far as their own meals were concerned, Andriana cooked plenty of traditional Greek dishes. She grew her own herbs (mint, coriander, basil, parsley) in large wooden boxes in the backyard. The nearest shop for Cypriot food, e.g. couscous, was a Turkish grocery in Brick Lane, and there was a Jewish bakery at Mile End that provided yeast for bread-making.

Mary's first school was Redman's Road (infants), followed by John Scurr (primary) both in Stepney, and Morpeth Secondary Modern (on the Bethnal Green border). One memory at Redman's Road was the choice between being dosed with malt or cod liver oil, her choice being malt. At Coronation time, all the young students were presented with a white Coronation mug and a blue propelling pencil.

Saturdays were different from those of most other children. For Mary, Saturdays meant Greek School. Her mother took her every week on the tube to All Saints Church in Pratt Street, Camden, the nearest Cypriot church (or, rather, Greek Christian Orthodox) to their Stepney home, where she mastered the intricacies of the language along with other immigrants. Some time later, her father sponsored a Greek class on Saturday mornings at Redman's Road School, which survived for several years.

*Dad behind the counter of the Classic, 1950s. (Mary Pallicaros collection)*

At John Scurr, Mary remembers the headmaster, Mr Jones, who summoned her father to the school at one point to advise against Greek lessons, because it was too 'confusing' for Mary who was learning English at school. When Mary illustrated that she could easily distinguish between the two, the headmaster lost the argument. Mary would have grown up bilingual, anyway, partly because her mother only spoke Greek to her.

Another memory of John Scurr is of a holiday in an Isle of Wight hotel, with the headmaster in tow, and one bathroom for all the children. Summer holidays, however, were always spent in Cyprus in the '60s, in a one-roomed house owned by the family. Mary's time here would also include a week with one uncle in Nicosia and another in Larnaca and a few days at a family mountain home.

Local friends included Caroline from the Ocean Estate, and Lilian and Ivy, sisters from Mile End Place close by. They would spend hours on roller skates, or playing ball games in the large yard of the Classic. Another friend, and distant relative, was Yiannoulla Kourtoulou whose family lived above their own restaurant – Milwards – opposite the Odeon in Mile End Road. This building had a flat roof, ideal for playing and for making daring jumps to adjacent roofs and it seems that the snooker hall next door was one haunt of the Kray brothers.

Sundays, for Mary, meant another visit to church in Camden Town. Occasionally, this would vary – with a visit to the cathedral in Moscow Road, Bayswater, although this meant sitting through a very formal three-hour service. There were plenty of relatives to visit at weekends, and a lot of Greek weddings, although her dad would always be a late-comer for these because he could only go after the restaurant was closed.

*Mary and her dad outside the Classic, 1960s. (Mary Pallicaros collection)*

*Mary and cousin, 1960s, on a flat roof at the rear of the Classic. (Mary Pallicaros collection)*

*Mary (right) in Mile End Hospital, 1959. (Mary Pallicaros collection)*

At the time of her Eleven Plus examination, Mary was seriously ill – with double pneumonia. She was treated in the Jewish hospital in Stepney Green. Thus her next move was to secondary school, where, in her first year, she again had health problems. The onset of nephritis (a kidney complaint) meant spending a lot of time in and out of Mile End Hospital.

Ill health didn't prevent her getting her Greek O Level in her third year – which meant that Greek School could end. Because Mary spent a lot of her spare time studying, to catch up, she went on to do well enough in her remaining O Levels to take on A Levels at Morpeth, and she was Deputy Head Girl in the Lower 6th, and Head Girl in the Upper 6th. The '60s, therefore, did not swing quite as much for Mary as for others, but she certainly does not feel that she missed out – far from it. The headmaster's wife, Mrs Mitchell, who was involved in school life, chose Mary as the school's representative to attend such functions as Inner Wheel meetings – and Mary also has fond memories of pirate radio and Sunday afternoons with the Top Twenty.

The ill health of her grandmother meant that Mary's father needed a passport to visit Cyprus and he approached Canon Young, rector of the nearby St Dunstan's Church, to sign his application. Father Young was the man on the receiving end of a supply of vegetables from Gregory every Harvest Festival, and was more than happy to return the favour.

Further education was always a first choice in 1965, but before this Mary had to get her Biology O Level (in six months) as she had omitted sciences from her O Level choices. The year 1965 turned out to be memorable for two other reasons: one sad memory – the death of the Head Boy at Morpeth, William Ray, who had a heart attack during the Easter holidays

*Mary teaching at Sir John Cass, 1969. (Mary Pallicaros collection)*

– and one happier one: passing her driving test (although there was no need for a car and nowhere to put one!).

Mary attended Phillipa Fawcett Teacher Training College in Streatham for two years, with another two years at the Institute of Education in Gower Street and the LSE in Houghton Street resulting in the BEd she wanted (in education and business studies). These colleges were all accessible by tube, and Mary always felt safe in and around her Stepney environs even when returning home late at night.

Her first teaching job in 1969 – Head of Business Studies – was at Sir John Cass's Church of England School in Stepney Way. In 1970, the GLC put a compulsory purchase order on the Classic (to widen the Mile End Road), a drawn-out issue resulting in a move to Finchley in 1973. Mary continued to teach at Sir John Cass until 1975, when she took up a deputy head-ship nearer home. Stepney students who knew Mary's background must have been greatly encouraged to see what they too could achieve with the right amount of application.

# ROSE PAYNE

## *Starting With Ten …*

By 1952, Rose's two older brothers had married and moved out of the family home, so when they moved to a four-bedroom flat in Malacca House on the Ocean Estate, Mile End Road, the family had shrunk to just eight. Rose, her remaining five siblings and her parents had more space in the fifth-floor flat than they had had in their Hackney house, with the added luxury of a bathroom.

Rose's memories of her mum are of her constantly cooking for such a large family, though she never used a recipe book or measured anything. She also remembers the pride she took in keeping the flat, and the approach, spotlessly clean. This was certainly a full-time job. Her father worked in the West End as a printer and a book-binder.

At the beginning of the 1950s Rose first met her future husband, William. She was thirteen and he was four years older. She met him again on the bus coming home from work a number of years later, but he had to do his two years National Service (in Sri Lanka) before they married in 1955. In the meantime, Rose and her friends enjoyed visiting Larkswood Swimming Pool (further East, in Chingford), and going to dance halls even further afield – in Tottenham or even as far as Hammersmith in West London.

When Rose and her family moved to Malacca House, Rose was working on the counter of a haberdashery in Stoke Newington, and she continued with the job after her marriage. The wedding was a large, traditional affair in St Dunstan's because Rose was the first girl to marry after five boys. The reception was on her original turf, at Hackney Lansdown Working Men's Club in Mare Street. Their honeymoon was spent in a caravan in Bournemouth.

Married life started in two rooms with her parents, less crowded as siblings gradually moved out. Socially, her husband liked dog racing, and the young couple would go along to the track at Clapton Pond, or, later, to Hackney or Walthamstow.

In 1960, Steven was born in Bancroft Road Hospital, and, although Rose stayed at home for a while, she was able, with the help of her mother and husband, to find an evening job at Lesney's in Hackney, the Matchbox toy manufacturers. She spent a number of years there, starting off by putting wheels on toy cars, and progressing to calculating the production staff bonuses. The company provided a bus to take staff to and from the factory.

Steven went to Ben Jonson primary school, starting there at around the same time (1965) that Rose and William secured their own (two-bedroom) flat in Malacca House, where they stayed until the 1970s.

The nearest park for the children was known locally as Shandy Park and was literally yards away from the flats. This not only had a paddling pool, it even had a park-keeper who kept the children – and the rubbish – in check. Steve had plenty of friends from the blocks of flats on the estate.

*Mary's nephew John in Shandy Park. (Ruth Payne collection)*

*Steve (front) in the local playground, 1960s. (Ruth Payne collection)*

Rose tells of an incident when Steve, in 1968, was standing on a chair looking out of the window – a favourite vantage point, apparently – at the Anchor and Hope pub opposite. He announced that he had seen a man shooting a woman, a 'story' which turned out to be true and which subsequently appeared in the local newspapers (eighteen-year-old Linda Pugh shot by her uncle).

By now, Rose was working six days a week at the Horse Race Totalisator Board then in Blackfriars (London EC4) where she used to take bets from 'Lords and toffs'. More than 100 people worked alongside her.

Before the end of the 1960s, the family were able to treat themselves to a holiday chalet at King's Holiday Park on Canvey Island, an area they knew because one of Rose's sisters had moved there. They went most Fridays in the summer for the weekend, and took Rose's mum along, too. When at home, Rose was a bit embarrassed if she heard anyone singing on the microphone at a local pub in Durham Row, as it seems the standard was not too high. Not that they spent much time in the local pubs, especially when young Steve became interested in football towards the end of the '60s.

He obviously shared this interest with his father, William, because William helped to run a boys' football club in the area, the Senrab Boys. Steve played football from around the age of eight, and the team played on Saturdays and Sundays, travelling far and wide, and trained during the week. There was a club-room which meant that the women-folk could join in socially. The club became quite famous, producing a number of professionals, at least eight of whom have become international players, including Ray 'Butch' Wilkins, MBE, and, more recently, John Terry.

# BETTY AND RONNIE SCHWARTZ

## *Mixed Feelings*

Unfortunately, Betty's memories of being brought up in Stepney are tainted with memories of anti-Semitism. Her father had a green-grocer's (Mark's) on the corner of White Horse Lane and Ben Jonson Road, and they lived above the shop, moving to the Ocean Estate (Anson House) in the early '50s. The parade of shops included a baker's, sweet-shop and chemist's, and Mark's was open seven days a week, meaning that they did not lead a strictly kosher existence.

It does seem as if the family were targeted. String was tied around their door handle and pulled in the middle of the night, a brick was thrown through the window at one point, and Betty, a small quiet child, was called names, chased, and threatened with a plank of wood. On one occasion, when carrying a box of matzos, she was insulted, grabbed and pushed, and her new coat with its Peter Pan collar was damaged. Although she told her parents, the people she accused denied her accusations, and Betty was not believed. Her brother, in some ways her opposite in that he was tall and gangly, was also bullied, and got into a lot of scrapes as a result. Even at grammar school, Betty can remember a swastika carved into her desk.

At home, her father was a pretty domineering character, an ex-Sergeant and desert rat, who was used to giving orders, and liked to shout. He did remember to buy flowers for his wife every Sunday, however, as some form of compensation. Betty's mother was a helpful neighbourly character, operating as a kind of local agony aunt for her customers.

Betty finds it amusing that she taught some of the local children to dance an Israeli dance in the grounds of the flats – the Hora – without their being aware of its Jewish roots. She and her brother also enjoyed holidays organised by the Country Holiday Fund, when they went on long hikes, singing as they walked (usually around Seaford in Sussex). It was during one of these holidays that she visited a farm for the first time – although even this happy experience was marginally tarnished when she fell into a cowpat when running from a bull, and everyone laughed at her. Amongst her favourite extra-curricular activities were her ballet lessons (at Toynbee Hall) and her membership of the Oxford and St George Club (Berner Street, since re-named) from the age of twelve, a Jewish club to which young Helen Shapiro belonged and which had a gym on its roof.

From the age of eight, Betty got the tea ready, and helped to light the fire with paper and wood. She enjoyed playing records in her bedroom while doing her homework. She remembers answering her Eleven Plus essay question by writing about 'An Invisible Cloak' – long before *Harry Potter*. It seems her dad was not impressed, however, and she recalls him raising his hand

*Betty and her brother Harold, 1950s. (Betty Schwartz collection)*

*Betty on Ocean Estate. (Betty Schwartz collection)*

to her after this exam, for some reason unsatisfied, a reaction which had an adverse effect on all her future exams.

Among Betty's memories of her dad and his business were of local burglaries. When Mark's itself was burgled, a dozen policeman turned up on the scene and revealed the names of the schoolchildren responsible. As a result, her dad visited the school and made the children go back to the shop, clean up the mess and run errands, ensuring that they didn't do the same thing again. Another memory is of her brother, Harold, age sixteen, watching two men removing all the goods from the next-door electrical shop one Sunday morning – their story being that they had to remove the goods so they could re-decorate the shop. Harold closed up the shop at lunch-time, but next morning found the police 'crawling everywhere' because the electrical shop's stock had been stolen: this time her dad, after hearing Harold's story, kept quiet – as did Harold.

*Mark's, Ben Jonson Road. (Betty Schwartz collection)*

*Ronnie selling linen in Wentworth Street. (Schwartz collection)*

Betty's first school was Stepney Jewish in Stepney Way in the '50s, and Raines Grammar School in Arbour Square in the '60s (yes, she passed the Eleven Plus). Although the family moved to Gants Hill ((Ilford) in 1962, Betty commuted to Raines. Early on, she was thrown out of the RE lesson when, as a well-read child, she questioned how you could believe Adam and Eve if you believed Darwin. The strict uniform included a bowler hat, and she had to wear the same gymslip for year on year, for so long in fact that at least one teacher described her as an urchin. Her grandmother (also on the Ocean Estate) knitted clothes for her where possible, but she finally got her first – memorable – off-the-peg dress at the age of thirteen.

Before moving house, Betty had a Saturday job in Samara's in Upper Street, Islington. For 12s 6d she made tea and cleaned the shoulders of rows of heavy barathea coats. On Sunday afternoons, her dad would often take the family (including cousins and various hangers-on) to Hampton Court in a Dormobile van which had orange boxes for seats. She was taken on a few holidays with her grandparents by 'charabanc' to Molly's Guest House in Cliftonville (Kent). Here, her brother collected crabs and eels which he put in a bucket, until the day someone wrapped an eel in his handkerchief and put it in his pocket – which, when he sneezed and put his hand in his pocket, caused quite a lot of excitement on the coach.

Betty's husband, Ronnie, is a Hackney lad, but worked the market at Petticoat Lane for thirty years from around 1958, selling linens on Sundays. He had other 'little earners' around Stepney – fly pitching in Roman Road market on Saturdays selling 'two pens for half a crown' or selling peanuts outside the Stepney cinemas. For the latter, he needed the protection of one of the Krays' henchmen because the pitches, and the trade, were considered profitable enough to protect. He has sold an eclectic mix of goodies over the years – from hula hoops in Club Row to home-made ice-lollies in London Fields. For selling black market tea, he was fined half a crown, a heavy penalty, but he got away with selling sugar during rationing. Around the time of the Coronation, he was making a good profit from selling plastic handbags shaped like Coronets for £1 each.

Socially, Ronnie also spent some time in Stepney. The Krays' club in Eric Street was a favourite haunt for snooker, and the open-air dancing in Victoria Park in good weather on Wednesdays and Saturdays was quite a draw, not least because of the presence of a live band. By the end of the '60s, although he had moved to Bow, he was still spending time in Stepney. His memories of the '50s and '60s, and of Stepney in particular, are much happier than his wife's.

# TERRY SHABI

## *Boxing and Barnardo's*

Although Terry describes his childhood in Stepney in the '50s as 'a normal East End childhood', I'm not sure this is strictly accurate. He is one of the seven children born to an African father and Welsh mother at a time when mixed race marriages were not at all common.

Terry's father was a professional boxer who came over to the UK in the late 1940s, marrying his Welsh bride (who was living in London) and making a home in two rooms on the top floor of 57 Lambeth Street, off Cable Street. The house was the only one left standing in the street after the war, looking out on to railway arches, but with just one shop – the CWS as it was then (the Co-op) – remaining at the end of the road. The remaining area was, literally, a bomb site, particularly memorable in Terry's eyes as the location for a really nasty accident when playing with his friend Robin. Their high spirits resulted in the remains of a vulnerable building collapsing and falling on Robin, who had to have both arms amputated.

As for Terry, he was born in Bancroft Road Hospital, and remembers being confirmed by Roger Royle, later Canon Royle and long-term radio presenter of *Sunday Half Hour* on Radio 2. (Roger Royle was also god-father for Terry's elder brother, Raymond).

He also remembers the Spartan facilities of that first 1950s home. The two rooms were shared with his older brothers and sister (two more sisters came along later), and he never got the hottest, cleanest bath water poured into the bath set up in front of the coal fire. This was reserved for the oldest son. By the time it was Terry's turn in the pecking order, the water was tepid and murky.

A bigger problem for Terry during his childhood was that his father did not leave his violence behind in the boxing ring. So it was a regular event for his mother to take him – and his siblings – to the Barnardo's home in Barkingside, Essex, quite a few miles away, for their own safety, escaping herself to one of her sisters (one close by in Old Montague Street, off Brick Lane, the other in Wales) until she felt able to return home. She was a seriously tough lady, although slight framed, having to tolerate racist comments outside the house and dodging blows inside.

The amount of time Terry stayed at Barnardo's varied from a month to over a year. When in Barnardo's, the children were split into different cottages, which were classified according to age. He started at Forget Me Not Cottage (with matron Mrs Pritchard), then Ivy Cottage (with Janet and Peter Knight) and finally Wild Violets with Mr and Mrs Creasey. Barnardo's had their own school, Mossford Green, which Terry attended when he was there, but when in Lambeth Street he attended Harry Gosling School, Henriques Street, and recalls that singer Frankie Vaughan was patron at the time. Most of his childhood holidays (in Bognor or Southend) were organised by foster parents, and most Christmases seem to have been spent at Barnardo's, too.

*Truman's Brewery, late 1960s. (Courtesy of Tower Hamlets Local History Library)*

Understandably, it wasn't unusual for Terry to be reluctant to return home, even when the 'coast was clear', but he was encouraged to do so as much as possible.

Meanwhile, his father was a regular church-goer, frequenting the Strangers' Rest Mission in The Highway, Stepney, on Sundays. He even assisted the mission – run by a Mr Hutchinson – financially when the building needed re-furbishing, but remained the only non-white face in the congregation.

When Terry did spend a weekend at home, his mother saw that they spent most of their time out of the house. There were markets in Brick Lane and Bethnal Green Road, and they could walk to the Tower of London which had a green area surrounding the buildings which was open to the public, with a small, man-made 'beach' lapped by the River Thames. He laughs about spending a few pence on *Topper*, *Beano* and *Dandy* or on a bottle of Tizer, 3*d* worth of chips or a handful of sweets, paid for by car cleaning or hedge cutting rather than with pocket money.

Interestingly, in spite of his ability to handle himself, Terry's father seems to have felt threatened when his grown-up nephews came to visit from Wales – they were teddy boys who stayed in Old Montague Street when visiting, and were certainly aware of the strained relationship at the Shabis' thanks to Terry's aunt Lucy.

'Honey Boy' Shabi made a comfortable living as a professional boxer throughout the '50s, with mostly local appearances, but later in this decade he got himself a 'regular' job working for local brewery company, Truman's, where he serviced machinery. Terry himself was never attracted to boxing, though his brother Raymond – encouraged by dad – did have a few amateur bouts in the '60s.

Around 1958, the Shabis' Lambeth Street home was the possible victim of an arson attack – regarded by the police at the time as a possible racist attack. Terry remembers the extending ladder, and a fireman appearing at the window – but no one was hurt, luckily, and the family were eventually re-housed in Finsbury Park, his father continuing to work with Truman's. He remembers his dad buying a motorbike in the '50s, with a Vauxhall Cresta not long after.

As an older Barnardo's boy, Terry spent some time at Fairlop School in Hainault, on the outskirts of East London, a residential placement. He and his brother, Raymond, often ran away, and were brought back by the police. The boys' dislike was in part a result of the stigma of being allocated free school dinners and having to wait in a segregated line at lunch-time before being served with what appeared to be everyone else's left-overs.

In 1965, Terry left Barnardo's, and went to a school in Islington as his family were now living in North London. For him, his time in Stepney was over, but his memories are clear, if not always rosy, and he has been a hoarder of memorabilia for the period ever since.

# PAT SHEPHARD

## *Outside Influences*

Pat is an Essex resident who began the 1950s in a prefab – in Treby Street, E3 – very soon moving to a top-floor flat in Ryder House in Colebert Avenue on Bancroft Estate. This was the first time Pat had seen a bathroom or experienced instant hot water. Her younger brother was born in Mile End Hospital in 1950 after the one-bedroom flat had been allocated, and trying to change the allocation was so difficult that Pat shared a bedroom with her brother until she was nineteen.

Her father, Walter (Cleaver), known as Jim, had been demobbed after serious injuries to his shoulder and face, resulting in hospitalisation in Italy. He managed to find work as a painter-decorator, and never spoke about his experiences (or at least not until just before his death) – a quiet man, bookish, and with little conversation and no propensity for affection. Pat can only remember a brief weekly conversation on Fridays (presumably pay day) when he would ask her to get his tobacco, for which she received 6d as a reward. Her mother was an early morning office cleaner in the City.

By 1950, Pat had moved from Cephas Street (infants) to John Scurr Primary. Mr Hardy, her class teacher, in the third/fourth year, took a parental interest in young Pat, and some of the other 'deprived' children, driving them in his little Morris to his home. This was the first time Pat had ever been in a car, and the first time she had seen such a comfortable house as the one he had in Ilford, with a piano which his daughter played. He was a special influence, encouraging her to strive for success.

When not at home or school, Pat enjoyed venturing a mile or so to the Tower of London, where, for perhaps 1d, she could spend the day within its historic walls. There was a small beach alongside the river and stately ravens to admire or annoy. Victoria Park in Bethnal Green was in the opposite direction, but, again, a whole day could be spent in its environs. Plus, there was room in the grounds of the flats to meet up with local children, and they could sit on the steps chatting until late at night, without fear and without parental concern. Even regular trips alone on a bus (the 106) to Canning Town to pay the hire purchase instalments to a furniture shop was not regarded as anything out of the ordinary, even though she was only nine or ten at the time.

Meanwhile, in Colebert Avenue, the Cleavers had made friends with the generous Bellingers. Mrs Bellinger was a cashier in a butcher's in Bethnal Green Road, and, when Pat went to get the family's meat, she always gave her far too much change, knowing that their funds were very limited. The Bellingers also took Pat on holiday a couple of times, once to a bed-and-breakfast in Jersey, the aeroplane trip being another first for Pat.

She did have a holiday abroad before this, however, thanks to a youth club in Morpeth Street. The club members went to Rimini (Italy) by train, starting out at Bethnal Green station

*Pat as a schoolgirl. (Pat Shephard collection)*

*Pat outside Ryder House. (Pat Shephard collection)*

– and although she slept in her clothes for two days *en route*, this was quite an event for a girl who had never been further than Canvey Island or Ramsgate up to that point.

Less pleasant were her mother's noisy siblings (ten of them) who liked to take beer back to the flat after the pubs had shut so they could carry on drinking – although this did have the bonus of plenty of empty beer bottles that Pat returned in exchange for a few pence.

The Coronation in 1953 was celebrated with a street party – because of the rain, the tables were laid out under the railway bridge across Malcolm Road to give the maximum cover. Mementoes included a decorative Coronation tin of sweets and a souvenir spoon. At school, the pupils in Pat's class had made a frieze to celebrate the Coronation, and this won them a prize. Soon after, the whole school were treated to a coach trip to see *The Ascent of Mount Everest* and the film of the Coronation at the Odeon in Mile End Road.

Having passed her Eleven Plus at John Scurr, Pat was encouraged to take the entrance examination to get into the Central Foundation School for Girls at Spitalfields, a prestigious E1 school. She passed the exam, and the daunting pre-entrance interview, meaning that her parents had to find the money for her uniform. Every item, including the green knickers with pockets and the brown socks, had to be purchased from Gamages, the Holborn store. Luckily, by then, her father had secured more regular employment with the Post Office at their sorting office in Mount Pleasant in the City.

The Central Foundation was a ward school, with parents being mainly comfortable professionals, including diplomats. Originally, it was built for children from poor families, their fees paid for by City merchants. Jewish children usually formed separate cliques, as did children from different social scales, and Pat is convinced that neither she nor any of the East End children at the school were ever invited to join the holidays arranged by the school. Her situation meant that the uniform her parents had invested in so heavily had to last her throughout her years here, with clever extensions added as she grew. Worse than that, with hindsight, was perhaps the fact that she was not offered the opportunity to go on to do A levels or to university, in spite of her obvious academic abilities.

At school – reached on a no. 8 bus – Latin was on the agenda, as was sewing and French, and the allocated homework was pretty intense. Miss Holt was a memorable, if strict, history teacher, with other teachers such as Miss Brown (who had fine long plaits) issuing reprimands for any deviation in uniform – if your cardigan sleeves were pushed up, for instance, you would be asked, 'Are you going to do the washing up?' The head, Miss West, always wore an academic gown and all the teachers were similarly garbed during school assemblies and other functions.

Other lessons which set the school apart were ballroom dancing, elocution lessons and deportment lessons, along with Greek dancing, which saw Pat hand-sewing pale blue lining material (the cheapest material in the shop) for the necessary tunic. School dinners were less memorable than might be anticipated, and the Jewish children had a kosher menu.

There was quite a lot of activity outside school premises – hockey in Regents Park (Central London), tennis at Belsize Park (North London), netball at 'Barmy' Park (Bethnal Green), and prize giving at Mansion House (in the City). Predictably, Pat couldn't afford the necessary sports equipment, and never owned a hockey stick or tennis racquet. These had to be borrowed from the school. Hockey shoes were made for her by her father (who in fact repaired all the family's shoes): adapted from old school shoes, with leather studs hammered into the soles. Similarly, a school friend, Irene (from Bethnal Green), adapted some white bridesmaid shoes, dyeing them and adding a wooden base, for the same purpose. In spite of such handicaps, Pat represented the school at netball.

By the time Pat was fourteen her mother was hospitalised long-term in Mile End Hospital following a hysterectomy with additional complications. This meant Pat had to take on the care of her younger brother, getting him off to school, along with the housework, house-keeping, paying the bills, doing the washing and ironing, and then spending her Saturdays doing the same thing for her two uncles in Bow – these bachelors having been reliant on her mother to 'look after them'. She also managed to visit her mother in hospital on a daily basis – and keep up with her homework.

In 1958, Pat left school. She went to work at Sun Life Insurance in the City, in the Actuarial Department. Soon after (in September, aged sixteen) she met her husband-to-be, Derek, who was in the merchant navy, and had accompanied his friend to one of Sun Life's company outings. Derek, seven years her senior, had been round the world twice and went on long trips for the New Zealand Shipping Company at a time when it took six weeks to get to Australia or New Zealand. This meant Pat only saw him every five months or so, although she wrote to him frequently while he was away. When Derek (from north London) did come home, they spent his five-month salary in the six weeks he was on leave.

*One of Pat's wedding telegrams. (Pat
Shephard collection)*

**Wedding Greetings Telegram**

258   WG4 10.26 PARKSTONE BH21

MR AND MRS D SHEPHARD 24 RYDER HOUSE TALBOT
AVE LONDONE1 =


BEST WISHES FOR YOUR FUTURE HAPPINESS =

DEREK YVONNE AND YVETTE ++

GPO

*Pat and her dad arriving for
the wedding. (Pat Shephard
collection)*

*Pat's wedding cake. (Pat Shephard collection)*

*Pat and Derek, post-wedding.
(Pat Shephard collection)*

As a teenager, with or without Derek, Pat enjoyed the jazz club scene in the West End or venturing to dance halls further afield (Tottenham Royal was popular). A Saturday job when at school – at Woolworth's, Gardiner's Corner – left her with enough savings to buy a Dansette record player when she was fifteen, thereafter funding the jazz records she liked: Ella Fitzgerald was a particular favourite. Jazz was something that she and Derek had in common.

Conscription for Derek ended in December 1960 (he was exempt from National Service anyway because of his stint at sea) and the couple decided to marry the following April. To seal the alliance, Derek splashed out on a diamond and had it made into an engagement ring (with matching wedding band) at Hatton Garden, and took Pat to see *West Side Story* on the West End stage. It wasn't quite that simple, however, because Jim Cleaver was concerned about Derek's swarthy appearance. Although this was in part due to the fact that he had spent so much time in the sunshine, Derek also had Mulatto ancestors. After the wedding had been arranged, Jim protested that 'Nobody asked me.' As a result, Derek was obliged to write to ask for formal permission to marry Pat – which was, perhaps reluctantly, given.

The white wedding took place at St John's on the Bethnal Green border, with a sandwich reception at home in Ryder House – though there was a rather splendid wedding cake. All the costs were taken care of by Derek. A little bit of help came from a white £5 note he had found in the pocket of his new wedding suit – from a mysterious benefactor. One of their wedding gifts was from John Langton, Pat's boss at Sun Life, a man who taught her a lot about the business world. As for a honeymoon, this was much cheaper – four hours at the Ideal Home Exhibition …

Derek's family paid for the work needed to make their first home, in Tottenham, liveable – it needed converting to a separate flat, to give them privacy from the elderly man who occupied the rest of the house. Unfortunately, they were evicted six months later, but they quickly found a fifth-floor flat in Waterloo Buildings in Bethnal Green Road. This was a bit of a step backwards, with no lift, one tap in the entire flat, and a toilet on the balcony next to the rubbish chute. It meant a weekly trip back to Pat's parents in Stepney for a bath.

When Derek's mother died soon after the wedding, he inherited a couple of hundred pounds, and with this money they opened their first bank account. A year or so later came another first when they bought a car at Mile End Garage (from Uncle Henry who worked there) – a Ford Anglia. Pat's father died of lung cancer in 1965, so Pat was then spending even more time in Ryder House – the place where her younger brother also lived and died, losing out to his own demon: alcohol.

For three and a half years, the couple saved for a bungalow of their own, built to their own design – on Canvey Island. It cost £3,150, and the mortgage – with a favourable interest rate – was 'sorted' by John Langton. Derek worked as a window cleaner for a while, starting off with downstairs windows while he served his 'apprenticeship'. He then applied for a job as a telegraphist with the GPO. Although this job meant long hours in central London, he learned how to type and it opened a lot of doors, including one at the Press Association later in the 1960s.

# EDIE and BRYAN SNOOKS

## *Who Needs Money?*

The home where Edie was brought up in Sidney Street was shared not only with her parents, brother, two sisters and another family upstairs, but the 'passage' was also a corridor to the clothing factory behind. While the two outside toilets in the yard sounds    almost    like a luxury, one was reserved for the factory staff, the other for everyone in the house.

Edie's dad was a docker at Wapping, and her mother an early-morning office cleaner. Although the cleaning work was mainly in the City, her mum also cleaned for the local Rabbi in Sidney Square and for some of the local shops, taking the children with her in the school holidays.

When the 1950s came along, Edie was at Rutland Street Primary School and still enjoying playing on bomb sites, which were far more exciting than boring grass. For pocket money, one of Edie's jobs was to clean the sink which was used for the art classes at school. On Fridays, after school, her older sister would meet her and they would share out her Spangles – Edie wasn't keen on the green ones. Then they would spend a bit of time either in Victoria Park or 'Barmy' Park.

A highlight of the school year was the annual day trip, usually to Littlehampton, when the whole school piled into half a dozen coaches. The cost of the trip (about 6s) was paid for in instalments.

Later in the '50s, when her brother was a bit older, one of the favourite parts of her year was Guy Fawkes time. He would go out collecting a 'penny for the guy', and spent all the money on fireworks, especially bangers. Edie herself was involved in collecting wood for the bonfire, and everyone joined in on 5 November.

Sadly, Edie's mum died at home in 1952. On this very day, Edie and her older sister had to go to the doctor's house in Stepney Way and tell him the news, so that he could visit the household and confirm her death. Her dad dyed all the household clothes black in the kitchen sink so that they would be suitably kitted out not just for the funeral but for a period of mourning. On the day of the funeral at St Augustine's, Edie got a ride in a car for the first time, and this little bit of excitement may have helped her deal with such a sad day. She was also pleased that her aunt bought her a new dress after the funeral, so that she had one dress at least that was not black.

Her youngest sister spent a lot of time with their 'nan' (in Sutton Street) for a few years to make it a little easier for the widowed father to manage. The family were regular church-goers, going twice a day during their mother's life-time, and once a day after she had died. They attended St Augustine's, now a part of the medical library at London Hospital. Now, to add to their busy day, the children also had to do all the housework, Edie's speciality being to clean the cinders from the open fire.

*Prefabs in Sidney Square. (Snooks collection)*

*Edie (left) and younger sister, Christine, Sidney Street, c. 1955. (Snooks collection)*

*Edie's dad and stepmother, 1950s.
(Snooks collection)*

*Bryan and his half sister, Rutherford
House, Brady Street. (Snooks collection)*

Their Coronation street party (in nearby Newark Street) was quite an active affair, with competitive races. By now, Edie had left primary school and moved to Dempsey Street School. The uniform was supplied via a charity, including the navy blue tie and beret – the beret being one of Edie's pet hates. Incidentally, free school dinners were supplied to families like Edie's not only during the school term, but also in the holidays from Monday to Friday. She and her siblings would eat at either Senrab Street School or Robert Montefiore, depending on which they were allocated. If Robert Montefiore, which involved crossing a main road, they would be accompanied by a teacher from that point to the school premises.

Edie had to leave school early every day, missing the end of lessons, to collect her sister who by now was at primary school. However, this particular issue was alleviated when her dad re-married. Her stepmother, Olive, proved a satisfactory replacement for the children, although they carried on doing the jobs they had grown used to – including cleaning the factory passage on Saturdays. It was Olive who introduced them to holidays – on Canvey Island.

Around 1957, Edie found a job at Wiggins, Thomas & Rudd, a leather tannery at Ratcliff Cross Street, near the Troxy. She worked in the office for several years, learning to type while there. With her first pay packet of £1.50 she had her ears pierced. The firm, small and old-fashioned, was very formal, with everyone addressed as Miss, Mr or Mrs. Edie's bosses, brothers, were called Mr Barry, Mr Horace and Mr Stanley (their first names).

Indirectly, it was Olive who introduced Edie to her husband, Bryan, also a local lad. Their 'courting' days were limited by finances, but there was always a romantic walk over Tower Bridge. They also spent time in the new local 'coffee bars', complete with juke boxes – Edie's favourite was Franks's Café in Sidney Street, while Bryan's was Val's in Brady Street. Bryan, it seems, kept promising Edie a game of bingo, but this never materialised.

They were married in 1961 at Stepney Town Hall, with a reception at The George in Jubilee Street. Their first baby, Bryan, arrived six months later. Edie had been dreading telling her very strict father about their plans to wed, and about the baby, but he took the news surprisingly well, and the special licence only took a week to organise.

For the first week of their marriage, they lived in their separate homes – Bryan in Rutherford House, Brady Street, with his grandma. And for that week, although married, Edie still had to be home by 10 o'clock. After that, the young couple moved to Cable Street for a year, into a flat above a cleaner's on the corner of Backchurch Lane, moving after that to Hackney. Incidentally, Bryan boxed for Brady Club as a youngster – a good idea for a lad always in trouble for fighting. The only fight Edie saw, however, was the one – at Hornsey Town Hall in North London – when he lost.

# CHRIS STERNSHINE

## *Diverse Communities*

The entry into the world of Chris and her twin, Vicki, at London Hospital, Whitechapel, was a cause of real celebration for her parents, who had lost earlier twins. Sam and Hannah Sternshine ran the Prince of Hesse on the corner of Plumbers Row and Fieldgate Street (now a car park) but were not the only publicans in the family – the previous generation and Sam's brother also featured. To mark the birth of the twins, they were presented with a Pekinese – Ching – by a customer.

The Prince of Hesse offered larger accommodation than many East Enders enjoyed during this period. There was a playroom for the children, with the rooms on different levels, and Chris recalls the dark hall, the impressive banisters, and the glass separating part of the stairwell from the pub which you could peer over if there were live musicians playing, skiffle bands being particularly popular at the time.

Opposite the pub was a kosher butcher, Barney Praag, who had two sons, one of them extremely keen on Airfix model kits. This interest attracted Chris and her sister briefly, but Chris was put off by the fly-paper over their eating area, which never seemed to be changed … Next door, Ray Snell did clothing repairs at home, and sold socks in vivid colours which she would display in a filthy window. This particular lady favoured newspaper as her carpet, and was also memorable for the chips she dished out, much to Hannah Sternshine's disapproval.

Employees of a neighbouring tailoring business (Woolf?) provided customers for the pub to add to locals and passing trade. Apart from tenements in Fieldgate Street, much of the area was dotted with bomb sites, which came in handy on 5 November, and also for the occasional visiting fair which might stay for a whole winter.

Robert Montefiore Primary School in Vallance Road was predominantly Jewish in the late '50s, so kosher school dinners and Hebrew lessons were taken for granted, as was leaving early on Friday for the Sabbath. On Saturdays, there was a children's service at Great Garden Street synagogue, and every other Saturday they were given a bar of Cadbury's chocolate. Chris managed to reduce her own visits down to fortnightly – to coincide with the chocolate. The Prince of Hesse would be open on Saturdays in spite of the kosher home behind the scenes, but would close on Jewish fasting days. Christmas was celebrated as well as Jewish festivals, with the customers in mind.

After school, it was a regular thing for the girls to go straight to the Brady Club in Hanbury Street, where they were provided with bread and jam. Mrs Green read nursery rhymes to the younger club members, and Chris attended ballet classes here, although, if you forgot your ballet shoes, you would dance bare-foot on the wooden floor and suffer the consequent splinters. Chris also remembers seeing Alfie Bass here, and Frankie Vaughan, who gave a concert. The

*Dad Sam behind the bar of The Prince of Hesse, 1950s. (Chris Sternshine collection)*

Brownies offered a passing interest, but the Brady was a favourite, especially as it arranged holidays, nature walks and such amusements as pressing flowers.

Hannah's mother lived with the family for some years (until 1956), and the twins would peek through her bedroom keyhole, fascinated by the long johns she wore – and by her speed with a treadle sewing machine. Sam's parents lived in a tenement block in Myrdle Street (a block they owned and rented out to immigrants at rock-bottom rents), where the family visited most Sundays. Other members of his family lived in Flower and Dean Street or in the tenements in Thrawl Street. The twins also had an aunt in Wentworth Street and cousin in Greatorex Street in a gated complex where she remains in her retirement. Several aunts were employed as barmaids at the pub.

The only time off for Sam Sternshine seemed to be to attend Masonic meetings, but he and his wife managed a regular Tuesday evening off when The Prince of Hesse was sold on by Charrington's in 1962. They moved on to the King's Head in Golding Street, a similar set up with a large flat over the pub, a second floor having been sacrificed during the war. The kitchen was big enough to house a television and armchairs as well as the more obvious essentials, and there was an open fire in the main lounge, rarely used after the first occasion, which covered everything with soot. Ascot heaters in the bathroom and kitchen provided hot water, and this was a comfortable place to live.

Soon after their move, Chris started at the local grammar, Raines Foundation, the same school her mother had attended (Hannah was actually born in a nearby pub, the Maid and Magpie). The main hall here displayed the school uniform, which was only available from Henry Taylor in Walthamstow, and this was also the place for school assemblies, although the Jewish children had their own assembly in a separate classroom, joining the non-Jewish pupils

*Chris (right) with Vicki, and Ray Snell, opposite The Prince of Hesse, c. 1955. (Chris Sternshine collection)*

*Chris outside the King's Head, c. 1962. (Chris Sternshine collection)*

*Chris the animal lover, Petticoat Lane, c. 1969.*
*(Chris Sternshine collection)*

for notices. Kosher lunches were provided at a nearby school, Rutland Street. With hindsight, there was some indication of anti-Semitism at the time from one or two teachers, with one example in particular. When Chris and her friend Valerie both complained of illness during the games period (at Fairlop) after the Easter break, the gym mistress marched them to the headmistress, proclaiming that 'the two Jews probably had too much at Passover'.

More amusingly, at her first music class, Chris was the only one without a recorder, on which her class learnt to play *Peter and the Wolf*. She spent music lessons listening instead. However, she was fascinated with musical instruments, perhaps dating from an early Christmas when the twins had both received drums as presents, or influenced by her mother's proficiency on the piano, which she played in the pub. A favourite haunt was Berry's in Whitechapel, and Chris did buy a harmonica here, although she'd always wanted to play the violin, so it was a rather inferior substitute. She was intrigued by a music teacher who lived opposite the King's Head, and also by the fact that one of her friends could play *Three Blind Mice* on the clarinet. At home, the family had a Dansette record player, with a stock of eclectic music as each of them had different musical tastes.

Chris was now spending a number of evenings at the Oxford and St George Youth Club (where she learned to play chopsticks on the piano), a huge place with dozens of rooms and numerous activities including an art class and quiz team. She and Valerie would venture as far as Bayswater Road (West London) for ice-skating, incorporating a visit to the Wimpy bar next door. Dances were advertised in the *Jewish Chronicle*, which could involve a lengthy journey on a Saturday evening – to Belsize Park for example.

In the pub, Sunday customers were different to the weekday trade. Being near to the Commercial Road, there were plenty of workers during the week from factories and wholesalers. Memorable characters included the bank manager with a bowler hat, and two Eastern Europeans: the Ukrainian who worked at Guy's Hospital and the baker from Poland, who communicated with each other in some cross-bred language across the two bars. The King's Head also had a regular clientele of prostitutes and pimps. Chris worked behind the bar from around the age of fifteen and was given a purse to look after for one such customer which filled up during the course of the evening, added to every time the prostitute disappeared with a customer, until it became difficult to close the clasp. These girls had a profitable 'business', arriving in fur coats, and trading not only locally but 'up West' in Shepherd's Market. Other regular customers were the dockers.

At weekends, retired dockers came into the pub, with local families, some of them from a new council block: Delafield House. They had the choice of three bars – two public bars (one with a juke box) and a saloon. The only real trouble in the pub came when drugs started to be used in the '60s, and it was this kind of 'trade' that could erupt into violence, even, on one occasion, during New Year celebrations.

Apart from working in the pub, Chris worked Saturday mornings and Thursday evenings in Woolworth's in the West End. She also tried Sunday mornings in Golding's, the baker's in Commercial Road, but this was not for her. Her sister worked in Supa Stores in Whitechapel, and also as a Saturday assistant in Kay's Hairdressers in Osborn Street. This latter episode prompted Hannah Sternshine to encourage her to open a salon, because she was keen to get out of the pub trade – but it didn't happen; nor did her idea of a mini cabbing company, a new trade at the time.

When Chris left school, she learned typing at Tower Hamlets College (then located in Dempsey Street School) for a year, continuing her (unpaid) pub work. As she was turning into a bit of a hippy, most of the people she met at the pub, however, were not on her wave-length, except for a brief liaison with one bearded type who liked live music. Her own favourite music during her flower power period veered towards the Mamas and Papas, Lovin' Spoonful, and Tiny Tim – although she also saw the Rolling Stones live.

Like many school-leavers, she started off as an office junior – after visiting the Alfred Marks agency. This job, at the Union Match Co. in Fenchurch Street, was offered to her after she'd been temping there, and she moved with them to Holborn for some seven years (into the '70s), starting off typing invoices and learning the switchboard, progressing through despatch duties and even art work for their advertising, before ending up as PA to their director.

Once she had spending power in the '60s, Chris spent her money on clothes (in Whitechapel Market and in the West End), at the Kardomah Coffee Bar (in Holborn) and on records from Paul's (Whitechapel). She also managed her first holiday abroad – to Belgium, with her sister and friends. The '60s was a time for 'firsts' not just for Chris, of course, but for vast swathes of the British population, especially those brought up in East London.

# RAY TABI

## *Sparing the Punches*

After a few years in Bethnal Green (Cookham Buildings in Old Nichol Street, home to a number of boxers in the '50s, including local legend Nobby Clarke) Ray's parents (French-Nigerian father and English-Irish mother) split up in the early '60s. As a result, he and his mum and six siblings moved into his aunt's three rooms in Brick Lane. This wasn't that far from his original 'playground' and he was able to continue contact with his friends, many of whom, like him, were interested in boxing from a very early age.

This early interest had been encouraged at a boxing club in Commercial Road over the Horse and Groom, run by the tough Burns family from Bethnal Green. The Vallance Youth Club in Chicksand Street and St Hilda's – or the Bruce – in Bethnal Green – provided other pastimes, including snooker, tennis, and, unofficially, three-card brag. Boxing and other sports were also offered at the Brady Youth Club in Hanbury Street, Whitechapel. Although this was primarily for local Jewish youth, a word in the right ear and a promise not to cause 'bother' meant that Ray and his friends could also utilise their facilities, including a bath, saving a visit to a public bath house.

When he left school in the '60s he worked, as well as lived, in and around Brick Lane. The area had a profusion of tailors and rag-trade businesses and Ray was able to move from one to another, acquiring a desirable skill along the way – the cutting of leathers and suedes. Billy Ocean, it seems, worked at one of these outlets in the '60s, if Ray's memory serves him correctly. (Ray was also introduced to 'an American guy' who had an aunt living in Watney Street, the guy turning out to be Paul Simon, who lived in England for a while in the '60s.)

The money that could be earned in this business by proficient cutters was well over and above the average, offering piece work of around 7s 6d for a jacket (with the potential to make up twenty in one day) and 10s for a coat. The trade was at its zenith in the '60s, supplying such retailers as Lord John's in Carnaby Street. This meant that Ray could afford to have a new suit made nearly every month, choosing the material himself. In one year alone, he recalls four mohair suits in a range of colours from kingfisher blue to navy pinstripe, two in worsted, and a Crombie overcoat, all made up by Brick Lane tailors. For shirts, there was Albert's in Aldgate (near Bloom's), who would make one up for you if you couldn't find what you wanted. Bethnal Green, or, more specifically, Blackman's in Cheshire Street, was the place for shoes.

Around 1964, Ray and his family (eight in all) moved to their own flat south of The Highway, their first with a bath. This was in Ross House, Prusom Street, which became quite a focal point for friends at Christmas, although their crowded parties were sometimes too crowded.

*Brady Boys' Club. (Courtesy of Tower Hamlets Local History Library)*

His social life extended to the West End clubs. The Last Chance in Oxford Street was a regular haunt, and, after a night in the West End, a favourite early Sunday morning location was known as the Comedown Café, off Petticoat Lane.

Locally, on Saturdays, Paul's was the place to buy every record in the charts, and it seems there was a Maltese-owned café in Hanbury Street which was strictly 'boys only' – a good place if you didn't mind your clothes smelling of the food for hours afterwards. Whitechapel Road generally was a good place to 'hang out' and meet up with friends, even on Sundays because Johnny Isaac's fish and chip shop was open. Not that Ray needed to eat out on Sundays as his mother was an excellent cook, and Sunday tea was always on the agenda with her excellent pastries.

By the end of the '60s, Ray was boxing again – mainly at the famous Repton in Bethnal Green – going on to win several divisional titles. Because he attended local charity gigs,

Petticoat Lane, 1960s. (Dee Gordon collection)

Danny Tabi (back row one from the left) and Peter Tabi (back row one from the right) with pals and newspaper vendor (with cap), Whitechapel, 1960s. (Ray Tabi collection)

*Ray and Harry Burns at the Frying Pan, Brick Lane, charity event, c. 1969. (Ray Tabi collection)*

he could hardly avoid the Krays, wearing their charitable, rather than villains', hats, and he remembers them sending him for twenty Player's cigarettes, with the instruction 'keep the change'. He actually visited both brothers (Ronnie in Broadmoor and Reggie in Parkhurst) later; not pleasant experiences.

But favourite memories of the 1950s and '60s are not necessarily of villains, of hard times, or of personal achievements, but more of local characters in and around Stepney – the rag-and-bone man, the Kia-Ora man, the Jewish busker who always sang 'My Yiddishe Momma', the 'mad vicar' who 'grassed up' the local villains, and 'Prince Monolulu' with the feathers on his head. They don't make them like that any more.

# BILL TAYLOR

## *Dockers and Drinkers*

At the end of the 1950s, Bill joined the merchant navy, when he was living with his family at Barkingside (Ilford, Essex), but very soon his parents decided to try the life of publicans. This was more his mother's idea, but it was also to get away from his father's ailing motorbike business. Fred and Beattie Taylor approached Mann and Crossman at Whitechapel, who offered them three pubs, and their choice was The Artichoke at Artichoke Hill, Stepney Highway. This was known locally as 'Cohen's pub' after a previous publican, an asthma sufferer who slept on the balcony at the back of the pub overlooking the docks.

The move took place when Bill was away at sea, but he remembers going along with his parents to the interview at the brewery. One of the questions he was asked was whether he would take the tenancy over when he had finished his naval service, and this he glibly agreed to do, knowing this was what they wanted to hear. For the next ten years, his parents ran a successful pub. The large flat above on two levels had rooms for Bill and his younger brother (Stan), and room for when his grandmother came to stay.

For the first few years of their tenancy, Bill spent a lot of time away at sea. But when he was home, his friends came mostly from the block of flats next door in Cuttle Close (since demolished). Large families inhabited the flats and many of them drank in The Artichoke. One good friend was local villain Bertie 'The Bomber' and his daughter, and Bill recalls that there was no real secrecy between friends as regards to their activity. It wasn't unusual for him to visit

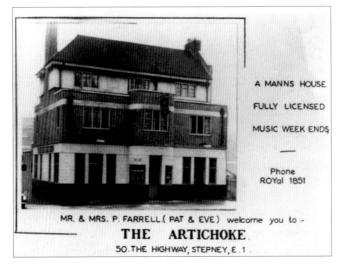

A MANNS HOUSE

FULLY LICENSED

MUSIC WEEK ENDS

———

Phone
ROYal 1851

MR. & MRS. P. FARRELL.( PAT & EVE ) welcome you to -
**THE ARTICHOKE**.
50. THE HIGHWAY, STEPNEY, E .1 .

*An advertisement for The Artichoke. (Bill Taylor collection)*

*Overlooking The Highway and Cuttle Close. (Bill Taylor collection)*

their flat, and find it strewn with, say, beaver lamb coats from a warehouse raid. Criminals and gangsters were one of the mainstays of the pub, and you always knew when they had done a job because they bought spirits instead of beer.

Not that there was trouble in the pub itself. The Taylors could not afford to get involved in what was going on under their noses as they could risk their licence, and they were both well able to deal with potential trouble-makers. Some of the Krays' henchmen became genuine friends. For instance, when Jacko (the dapper safe cracker) contracted cancer when in prison and was sent home to spend his last few days, the event was a rare opportunity to see grown men cry. Apart from such characters, the pub was busy with dockers at lunchtime and after work.

Bill didn't waste much time passing his driving test, and he and his mother bought a brand new Cortina Estate between them when they moved into the pub, replacing his first car, an old 100E Anglia. His mother had secured a driving licence before it was necessary to take a driving test.

By 1964, Bill felt that his own job was on its last legs, with the navy going over to containers, so he was interested in working in the docks. Quite a few of the bosses from the Port of London Authority drank in The Artichoke, and Bill was told there would be an opportunity some six months down the line. In the meantime, he went to work for the Keg Department of Mann & Crossman opposite the London Hospital, Whitechapel Road. The market here was busy when Bill had his lunch-time break, and he enjoyed the atmosphere.

It is interesting that numerous kegs and hogsheads of spirits were kept in a network of tunnels under the original London Docks, tunnels built by Napoleonic prisoners of war. Of course, such excessive opportunities for petty pilfering were not wasted on many of the men working in the docks, and much of it was effectively condoned. (Bill feels it was not that much different to naval men being able to bring home Levis and cigarettes which they could sell back

*Bill and pet behind the bar. (Bill Taylor collection)*

*Bill's parents, Beattie and Fred, behind the bar. (Bill Taylor collection)*

Telephone: ROYAL 2000, Ext 92/
Telegrams: POLAFEN, LONDON, E.C.3.

REPLY TO
CHIEF ENGINEER.

PORT OF LONDON AUTHORITY,
P.O. BOX No. 242,
TRINITY SQUARE,
LONDON, E.C.3.

Dear Sir,

I have to inform you that you have been engaged as

as DIVER on the Unestablished Wages Staff

of this Authority as from the 29th December, 1964.

subject to the receipt of satisfactory references and to the following

conditions:-

Pay £12.9.0 per 40 hr. week to £12.19.0 (AFTER ONE YEAR)

Hours of Duty 8 am. to 5 pm. MONDAY to FRIDAY (DAILY MEAL BREAK OF ONE HOUR)

Sick Pay     In accordance with the general regulations for the
             regularly employed unestablished staff applicable
             to this grade. No pay is allowed during the
             first six months' service but thereafter payment
             during certified sick absence is granted as
             follows.

             Full pay for up to six months and half pay for up
             to six months in any consecutive period of
             12 months, subject to a maximum of 12 months'
             sick leave in any period of 4 years.

Annual Leave 13 Working days per annum (with a proportion during
             the first leave year) in addition to Bank,
             Statutory and Proclaimed Holidays.

        Your contract of employment will be terminable at any time by you
by one week's notice and by the Authority by notice in accordance with
the following scale:-

Period of continuous service                    Period of notice

(calculated in accordance with the
provisions of the Contracts of
Employment Act 1963).

Less than 104 weeks                             One week

104 weeks or more but less than
260 weeks                                       Two weeks

260 weeks or more                               Four weeks

                        Yours faithfully,

MR. W. F. TAYLOR.
50, The HIGHWAY.
                        Divisional ....

*Bill's job offer from the PLA, 1964. (Bill Taylor collection)* in England.) It did mean that many of the men ended up drunk at the end of the working day, having to be collected on flat pallet trucks and dumped at the gates so that they weren't locked in overnight. Such a level of oblivion may well have made the task seem less tough than it was; lifting heavy sacks and boxes all day was hard and tiring work, with the added stress of the dockers not knowing from one day to the next if there was any work for them – they had to hang around at the gates at the beginning of the day to find out.

Bill joined the PLA as a diver in 1964; this job, too, was no cushy number. It was in the days of hard-hat diving, with woolly trousers, jumpers and socks worn under the diving suit, a breastplate and weighted belt added, finished off with lead boots – but no gloves because of the need to feel under the mud – looking for spillages from crates, or even bodies (before the River Police took over this latter duty). The punts took a chief and an assistant diver to the required part of the Thames, and air was supplied to their helmets through a tube by two men operating a pump, with a second 'pipe' for communication. The divers were also responsible for making sure the locks and sluice gates were clear, their role eventually taken by frogmen with their own air containers. When Bill's diving position came to an end, he moved on to working in the maintenance department, and became a shop steward.

There was some time left for Bill to socialise in the '60s. Bill would cross to another part of Stepney (Sidney Street) and another pub also called The Artichoke, and meet up with his friends before going on to a party or a dance. He and his friends favoured a sharply suited look – sharing common ground with Mods – and Bill had his mohair suits made at a tailor's opposite the London Hospital. Smart dress was regarded as essential for a night out.

By the end of the '60s there was a lot of change in the air, and the Taylors moved out of Stepney in 1970. Bill himself had been offered either a job at Tilbury or redundancy when the St Katharine's Dock closed in 1969, following the closure of the East India and the London Docks, and he chose the redundancy. The Artichoke's trade was beginning to suffer after the drink-driving laws were brought in and with the closure of the docks, so it seemed a good time to escape into nearby Essex and into the garage business.

# BARRY THURLOW

## *More Pubs*

Barry and his mother and Polish stepfather (originally Count Wolozynski, a refugee) settled in Peabody Buildings in John Fisher Street by the early 1950s. The small family had not one but two flats, a one-room (no. 42) flat used for the main bedroom, and a two room flat (no. 43) which provided a kitchen/lounge and a bedroom for Barry. There were toilets on their top-floor landing and a large washroom on each level of the block, which was around eight storeys high.

Barry's stepfather was a life-long gambler, and, unusually, a lucky one. He won enough money in a card game around 1953 to buy the Queen's Head in Fieldgate Street, behind London Hospital. This pub had been run by Barry's grandparents who moved to another pub at the Elephant and Castle (South London). This had more room (upstairs) for the family, a great improvement on Peabody Buildings: three bedrooms and a large lounge (originally two rooms).

The day of the move sticks in Barry's mind. His parents had intended to surprise him, taking him to his new home straight from school, but they missed him and he made his way home to his old address to find the flat empty and no sign of them! The neighbours confirmed that they had moved, sending Barry into floods of tears, until his stepfather came looking for him.

Through the 1950s and early '60s, Barry was going to Sir John Cass School (primary and secondary) at Aldgate, quite a prestigious institution. Teachers here had a reputation for being strict, and the uniform allowed for no variations such as not wearing the cap or adding turn-ups to the trousers.

George and Eileen (his parents) were ideal publicans. George was a large man, an ex-wrestler and ex-boxer, with a large personality. As for Eileen, she preferred the life to previous petty jobs – as a seamstress, or selling cakes in Dalston for a Polish friend with a Nigerian wife. George had been a merchant seaman and could handle the variety of customers that frequented the pub: policemen and businessmen, families, villains (such as Jacko, the safe blower), and residents of the local hostel – although these were in fact mostly working men. This motley collection had the potential for disaster, but George had the knack of sorting any trouble before it made any headway – he was even known to turn the Krays away, very politely, because of their reputation, with no apparent comeback. Barry's 'Uncle George' turned out to be George Cornell, the villain gunned down in the Blind Beggar in 1966 by Ronnie Kray because he'd called him a 'fat poof'.

The pub was known as 'George the Pole's' ('where the vodka flows like the Danube' said one pub guide) and was very profitable. George, however, was happy to spend the profits on his customers – if they bought him a drink, he would return the favour. If they had one drink too

*Peabody Buildings, John Fisher Street, Whitechapel. (Courtesy of Tower Hamlets Local History Library)*

*The Krays. (Dee Gordon collection)*

many, he would call them a taxi and insist they leave their car behind, and he would provide free food on the pub counter – anything from salt beef sandwiches to hot dogs or anchovies, catering for all tastes. He also provided entertainment other than the pub's juke box and television – Eileen was a renowned singer, the piano attracted local musicians, an accordionist would be playing, or there would be a performance from a skiffle group. Even after the pub had closed, there would be 'afters'. There was also betting and drinking through the afternoon.

George Wolozynski could, and did, command respect. He would lend money to his customers knowing that a) they would spend it in his pub, and b) they would always pay him back. He invested money in local businesses, helping out where he could, and employed quite a few staff. Barry was also involved: he would help out before school, bringing crates up from the cellar, cleaning bottles and stacking shelves. There was plenty of pocket money to be earned.

As Barry grew up, he became a regular at the Oxford and St George's Youth Club (at the Bernard Baron Settlement in Henriques Street). This was primarily for the local Jewish youth, but he was only questioned about his religion when he tried to join the All Jewish Youth football team – which was denied him. He did join their football club, though, and took part in the boxing. The premises were open six days a week for boys and girls, with a disco on Wednesday evenings, and the football team kept him busy playing local league matches on Hackney Marshes and other East London locations on Sundays. Weekends away were also organised, and there was even a trip to Switzerland which was paid for in weekly instalments. Barry met his future wife, Karen, at the club in 1962.

The '60s Mods versus Rockers phenomenon was different for Barry because he was, essentially, in both camps. He had an Excelsior two-stroke motorbike which he wore with suede boots and a string tie, and he also had a Vespa scooter. His parents did not approve of either

*Barry riding a stuffed horse on a rare holiday, 1950s. (Barry Thurlow collection)*

*Royal London Hospital, 2009. (Dee Gordon)*

mode of transport, so the vehicles were kept at a friend's house, but taken out at the weekends especially if there was a Mod/Rocker gathering at Brighton or another seaside location.

On leaving school, Barry went into the printing trade, working in Stratford (E15) before he got married, and in Old Street (EC1) afterwards. He also worked a couple of nights a week in the pub for his parents, as did Karen, although at some point she did have an independent job sewing on buttons for a friend's business in Bethnal Green.

In 1963, Barry and Karen had an early marriage at Poplar Town Hall, prompted in part by her pregnancy. For this she wore a pale blue suit with a mink collar. The year they got married was also the year Barry borrowed £100 from George to buy a 1958 black Morris 1000 – repaying the debt by working in the pub.

They lived with Karen's parents in Bethnal Green for a few months until after baby Leigh was born, and then moved into the flat over the Queen's Head. This was a temporary stop-gap until Leigh was five months old, at which time Eileen announced 'pack your bags, you're moving out.' It transpired that she had paid the £50 key money they needed for a flat across the road in Fieldgate Mansions. These flats were as old as Peabody Buildings, but low-rise. The young family were on the first floor, and there was a yard at the back for the dustbins and washing-lines. Their flat comprised bedroom, living room, kitchen, a small Ascot for hot water, and a toilet 'off the kitchen'. It also had a fitted bath which took up so much room that they removed it, using the one at the Queen's Head instead. The necessary furniture had been bought with money from a savings club.

Karen reminisces that Barry's mother was the mother-in-law from heaven. She would cook meals for them and send them over, and she would let them have enough coal for their fire from her own supply.

George was also quite a benefactor. He would pay Barry to drive him and his friends to the dog tracks twice a week and collect them afterwards. For this task, which meant driving to Hackney Wick, Charlton (in South London), Clapton or Haringey (both East London) he would be paid between £10 and £15, a generous settlement. It did not mean George deserted his customers, though, because he would be back in the pub by 10.30 p.m. As for Eileen, she would get a taxi if she wanted to do some shopping, even to the West End, but the everyday shop was done by pub staff. The couple rarely went out together, and their chosen work-load also meant that holidays were out of the question.

The Thurlows' second daughter, Jackie, was born in 1965 in the East End Maternity Unit in Commercial Road. By switching the use of bedroom and living room, and adding bunk beds in the bedroom, the family managed in the flat until offered a bigger place on the Isle of Dogs in 1968. The carpets and extra furniture they needed for this flat (a high rise) was paid for by George, in a shrewd move. He got £200 for the fixtures and fittings in Fieldgate Mansions from the next tenant, although the flats were actually owned by the hospital. It seems that the hospital, when told, did not 'mind a bit' – perhaps because so many of the staff knew, and liked, George the Pole.

It is interesting that, in later life, Barry not only turned down his step-father's offer of his own pub, but he became tee-total. Pubs were not for him, not on either side of the bar.

# RUTH TYLER

## *Family Life*

Barnes Street, off Commercial Road, was a typical Stepney Street with its rows of brick-built terraced houses, its tarmac road which few cars ventured across, and a factory (for cork) on the corner. In 1950, you could find Ruth here with her younger sister Joyce, her Nan Dyball, mum Ruth, and dad George. It was an unusually roomy house which Nan rented from the Byford Brothers, well-known local landlords. This meant Nan (mum's mother) could have her own upstairs space, i.e. living room, bedroom, and even her own kitchen on the landing.

However, pretty much everyone lived in the large downstairs kitchen with a big coal fire in winter. On bath nights, the side of the tin bath used to get red hot beside this fire. The outside toilet was at the end of a paved yard, as was dad's aviary with his budgerigars. Next door lived 'Nan' Hadley, who had a stable with a horse named Dolly. The horse used to pull cart-loads of fruit and veg to Old Road Market for her daughter's (and son-in-law's) stall. 'Nan' Hadley earned a little money in the evenings selling peanuts outside the Ben Hur cinema.

The weekends would often start with Saturday morning pictures at the Troxy in Commercial Road. This was the day that Ruth's extended family gathered round, George and Ruth both coming from big families. There was a lot of cooking going on, card games, and a piano for home-grown entertainment. On Sunday afternoon, a man with a horse and cart came around selling shell-fish, jellied eels, and Ruth's own favourite: pickled herring.

Every Tuesday evening when the girls were small, their mum went to see the speed-racing at West Ham. She used to go on the back of a motorbike, accompanied by her sister and friends, while dad did some baby-sitting. She was a great enthusiast. On summer evenings, Ruth and her cousins would play rounders, skipping and tops in the street. Other local facilities included Shadwell Park with its ponds and paddling pool. As a youngster, Ruth also had piano lessons from a lady in York Square (paid for by Nan Dyball), but it was never her favourite way of passing the time.

At the end of nearby Aston Street was St Mary's and St Michael's Church, bombed during the war. The annual May Day Parade from here was quite a special occasion. This was the venue for Sunday school for about thirty local children until it eventually fell down in the '50s, when the children switched to St Dunstan's. The priest, Father Young, had connections of some kind with the London Palladium, which meant that whenever the locals had a bazaar at Christmas or a fête during the summer, he was in a position to call upon one of the stars to open proceedings. Such gatherings took place at Senrab Street School, and the stars included Johnny Ray, Dickie Valentine, Shani Wallis and Frankie Vaughan (who was also connected to the local Brady Jewish Boys' Club). If you attended St Dunstan's Church, you could also join the Arbour Youth Club, and Ruth played in their netball team. This involved travelling around London for matches, usually on Saturday mornings.

*Joyce (left) next to Ruth, with local friends, 1950s. (Ruth Tyler collection)*

Ruth's father was a lorry driver (for BRS) right through the 1950s and '60s, and her mother worked in a cardboard box factory at Glasshouse Fields, where she folded the boxes. Nan Dyball worked in the ladies' rest room at Shadwell station at the end of Watney Street. She had a room with a big fire in and used to make tea for all the station workers when she wasn't cleaning. Any spare time she had was used to crochet mats and accessories which she sold to a shop in Commercial Road. The little bit of money she earned would be passed on to her two granddaughters every week in the form of pocket money, and she was also on-hand to baby-sit when needed.

Infant school and junior school for both girls was Caley's in Aston Street. Ruth recalls that the semolina was so disgusting that it put her right off school dinners altogether, so she went to a friend of her nan's at lunchtime until moving on to grammar school. One tragic incident from her time there sticks in Ruth's mind – when two brothers in her class were drowned in the bath by their mother following a breakdown in her marriage, the mother then committing suicide. In the early '50s, Clement Atlee was a school governor, and he came to prize giving when Ruth was about ten, presenting her with a prize – a book on fashion through the ages. He was the local MP at the time.

*The May Day procession,*
*Aston Street, 1950s.*
*(Ruth Tyler collection)*

*Ruth and Derek in their backyard, Barnes Street. (Ruth Tyler collection)*

*Derek with the Sunbeam Rapier in Barnes Street, 1962. (Ruth Tyler collection)*

*Wedding day at St Dunstan's, 1965. (Ruth Tyler collection)*

The family's first television, a small Bush, was purchased just after Christmas in 1952 – they bought it on the 6 February, the day King George VI died, and the BBC (the only channel) promptly went off air for two weeks out of respect! The following year, for the Coronation, the local street party was in York Square Park. Entertainment included a fancy-dress competition, with Ruth dressed as a hula girl, and Joyce as the Queen of Hearts. As part of the Coronation celebrations, the Canadian Mounties landed at East India Dock and rode in their red uniforms along the Commercial Road. Hundreds of locals lined the route to see them, but some of the younger ones were disappointed because they had been expecting to see Renfrew of *Renfrew of the Mounties*, a popular television series at the time.

At the end of the '50s, Ruth remembers Barbara Windsor being in the Watney Street area to film *Sparrows Can't Sing*, using the local school as one of the locations.

Christmases in the '50s were busy, with the family arriving *en masse*. Men would sleep on the floor, women and children in all the available beds. But there was room for a large Christmas tree, and one uncle always dressed up as a clown and invented brilliant games for the children, another uncle playing the piano, not that well, perhaps, but enthusiastically. One Christmas Eve her father and his brother-in-law came home with a doll and a Silver Cross pram for Ruth's Christmas gift, but, having stopped off for a few seasonal drinks *en route*, they fell up the stairs, and the doll was smashed – though the pram survived. The noise woke everyone up, and the two men were given a good talking to by Nan Dyball.

As for holidays, the main emphasis was on hop-picking at a farm in Tenterden in Kent. The lorry would park up in Barnes Street, and the family would load up every possible thing they might need for the six weeks when the schools were closed – including mattresses. Mum and the girls spent the whole six weeks there, with George joining them at weekends. This was really roughing it, with old barrels used as toilets, but it was enjoyable work in the open air with family and friends. Before returning to school, there would be a couple of weeks at a bungalow in Herne Bay, which belonged to a friend of Nan Dyball. Ongoing memories of these holidays are more mixed – Ruth loved the adjacent field of marguerites, but hated the resident goats which were rather too fond of her long plaits and ribbons.

Both sisters passed their Eleven Plus and went to Coborn Girls' Grammar School in Bow. One teacher whose memory lingers on is Mrs Bennet(t) who taught French – with a Welsh accent. The headmistress at Coborn was particularly strict, ensuring that any girl passing her in the hall would stand to attention. When mini-skirts became fashionable in the '60s, the head made pupils kneel to make sure their skirts were not too short. The boys at nearby Tredegar Square School (an ancient building, dominated by dark wood) would join the girls when it came to putting on school plays such as *The Mikado*, so the girls didn't have to play the male roles. It was at Tredegar that prize givings were held, attended by all the parents, as it was a bit bigger than Coborn. Another, adjoining, school, Malmesbury Road Juniors, housed the dining room for the girls at Coborn, the meals being a great improvement on those at Caley's.

To get to Coborn meant either two buses, or, more often, a combination of a bus and a walk (past the People's Palace in Mile End Road, now part of Queen Mary's College). The uniform comprised a navy blue pinafore dress with a blue-and-white check shirt, navy blue beret with a badge, and a blazer, with lisle stockings. On leaving school, all the girls threw their berets on the school railings as a celebration.

Ruth finally shed her uniform in 1959, and found a job in the City with Lloyds of London, working in the policy signing office dealing with claims. The location, near London Bridge, meant that she and her new girl-friends could sit by the River Thames at lunch-time, or walk around the green outskirts of the Tower of London. One day per week, they would walk up the 300+ steps of the Monument as a form of exercise. The job itself paid £7 6s per week and, although the punch card system she had to use was not an exciting way of earning a living, Ruth stayed there until 1966, commuting (until her marriage) by steam train from Stepney East (now Limehouse) to Fenchurch Street, and then usually walking the rest of the way.

After work, the girls went dancing a few miles from home – Ilford Palais, Tottenham Royal, Tottenham Court Road Astoria, and including the Lyceum when Joe Loss was playing, someone Ruth's dad had gone to school with (in Brick Lane). On Saturday afternoons, she would buy material in The Waste, Whitechapel, and make a skirt on the treadle they had at home, wearing it the same night to go out. On Sunday mornings, Ruth would visit her Nanny Kidd in Shoreditch and, on the way home, would stop at the record stalls in Petticoat Lane. She also bought records more locally, at Young's in Commercial Road. The gramophone in Barnes Street would be called into service to play the 78s that she brought home.

As for Saturday nights, once she was working, these would usually start off in an East End pub – the Blind Beggar being a favourite – followed by a party. One party she went to with a girl-friend a bit farther afield – at the Elephant and Castle in South London – left them stranded without transport, until some friendly local police stopped in their Black Maria and took them all the way back to their doorstep. They had to keep very quiet all the while so that nothing could be picked up on the vehicle's intercom, and, although very grateful, they were also a bit worried that the arrival of the police vehicle would be spotted – and misinterpreted – but they got away with it.

It was at the Blind Beggar in 1962 that Ruth met Derek. He lived in Chingford and worked at Hilger and Watts, the Debden scientific instrument makers. This meant that he could afford a car, and could pack quite a few girls in to take them to a party, leaving his friends to follow in taxis. The young couple progressed to seeing stage shows in the West End, and were fans of live music. However, after saving up the money for the engagement ring, Del announced that he had to replace his car, which had broken down, so the money went instead on a pale blue and black Sunbeam Rapier. So no engagement ring for Ruth … though Del made up for it later with an eternity ring.

Del and Ruth married at St Dunstan's in 1965, with a reception at the Sailors' Club at the end of Salmon Lane. The stunning wedding dress, complete with guipure lace and bustle, was a wedding gift from a cousin of Ruth's mother who worked for Ellis's Bridal Wear near Aldgate East station. They had a live band at the reception, with a cake made by an uncle who was a professional caterer. Even the pouring rain didn't spoil the day – or the wedding photos. For their honeymoon, they flew to Jersey from Gatwick in a little Heron, which involved climbing over the wing structure. This was the first time Derek had flown (Ruth had already had a holiday in Jersey) and must have been a bit daunting. On board, coffee was provided by the hostess from a flask. They survived this primitive experience and settled in Chingford for a few years before moving to Canvey Island.

# DEE WOOD

## *Those were the Days*

Although Dee vaguely remembers living with her grandmother (in Langdale Mansions, Cannon Street Road), her first family home was a flat in Redclyf House in Cephas Street, part of the Bancroft Estate. She, older sister Marcia and parents were there briefly, on the ground floor next to the lift, and this was where a party was held for the Coronation – under cover in the long sheds at the bottom of the flats, usually reserved for prams and other storage.

She started very young at Cephas Infants (well before the age of five) before moving prior to 1955 to Syon House in Rutland Street (near Sidney Street) when she moved to Rutland Street Primary. This was soon after her brother Alex was born – for which event she stayed overnight with her 'Auntie Iris' close by. The midwife came in on a daily basis after his birth, as it seems her mother had had quite a difficult time, and this particular lady is remembered for her kind gesture of buying Dee a doll when she broke hers when in a temper.

Syon House was a brand new three-bedroom flat with central heating, hot water, and laundry room on the ground floor with large washing machine and even larger drier. At this point, Dee's grandmother came to live with them. The play area for the local children was called the Debris, but it took a few years for Dee to realise what this actually meant: it was, of course, another bombsite. An early memory of Syon House (*c.* 1957) is of walking to see her dad's mother in Great Gardner Street, quite a walk away, a regular Sunday morning event – except on this occasion, a heavy smog came down in the area so dense that by the time she got to Whitechapel Post Office, she couldn't see more than a yard ahead and stood frozen to the spot, completely losing any sense of direction. Luckily, her father went out looking for her, calling her name. She can still feel the enormity of the relief at hearing his voice.

Rutland Street Primary had quite a high population of Jewish pupils, and followed some kosher guidelines when it came to school dinners – no milk in the custard, for example, meaning that, to Dee, it was bright yellow, semi-transparent, with an unpleasant taste. She also disliked semolina and rice pudding, which she was made to eat, and the dislike lingers on. Her first teacher was Mr Cohen, and the school had Hebrew classes, although Dee never managed to learn to read the language. They were not an orthodox family, although they did draw the line at bacon and pork, especially in front of her grandmother.

Her father worked in Ellis & Goldstein, the tailor's in Brick Lane, learning a range of different skills there. Her mother was employed in a biscuit factory, and brought home broken biscuits on Fridays, but over the years she had other jobs, such as selling fruit and sweets at a kiosk on Fenchurch Street station. She was very house-proud, changing the bedding and cleaning the oven every Thursday.

*Redclyf House, unchanged in 2009. (Dee Gordon)*

In his spare time, her father liked to spend time with Sid Frieze (*sic*) who ran the local betting office from his home nearby – not something of which her mother approved. Although Dee's father had a bit of a temper, and there was often tension between the parents, he could make her feel special just by taking her to Victoria Park at the weekend for a few hours.

Saturdays were shopping days, with food bought at Watney Street market in the morning or Whitechapel in the afternoon, and a visit to the butcher in Cambridge Heath Road. Dee's mum could rustle up meals from cheap ingredients – stuffed hearts with gravy, or a rolled and stuffed lamb joint. But she didn't usually eat with her family, claiming not to be hungry – but probably not wanting to deprive them of the nutrition on the table. Toys were not something the family spent money on, although Alex did have a rifle one Christmas which broke when it was used to try and deflect a snowball and hit the floor instead – Dee's attempts to repair it with tape did not go undetected.

When it came to taking the Eleven Plus, Dee was so nervous she got shingles. Her mother went in for the results, while she waited in the playground, and, although she hadn't passed, she

*Commercial Road, 1950s. (Courtesy of Tower Hamlets Local History Library)*

was offered a 'Governor's place', dependent on another test. She declined this offer, wanting to be with her friends who went to Robert Montefiore Secondary. On her first day, the building seemed large enough to get lost in, and the headmaster, Mr Rhodes Boynson, with his cape and his cane, was very daunting. He taught English, but with his broad Welsh accent and fast delivery Dee had trouble understanding him. She did pick up French quickly, however, but hated needlework, never getting to grips with the sewing machine – the only thing she made successfully was called a flump, a soft toy consisting of a head with feet.

By the age of twelve Dee started going to the Brady Club, but, at thirteen, she preferred the St George's Club, where she could spend time listening to music, make friends and learn how to paint her nails. She also started spending time with a cousin in Forest Gate, whose father was less strict than her own, meaning that they could stay out later. An early, Mod, boyfriend she met in Forest Gate was Tom, complete with parka and scooter. Her father insisted she wore a crash helmet, but she removed this as soon as they were out of sight of the flat: it was not a Mod trend. He ended up in prison, which reduced her to sobbing during one assembly. Later, she found out that he had been trying to get messages to her from prison, but both her dad and her uncle had made sure she didn't get them – perhaps luckily.

While at school, she spent rather too much time having crafty cigarettes in the boiler room, or sneaking out to buy chips or going to the Café Valencia in Vallance Road. This was near the sweet-shop where you could buy five Bachelors or just a single cigarette if your pocket money had run out. Extra money could be earned at her Saturday job at Jeffrey's (hairdressers) in Commercial Road and, apart from cigarettes, Dee would also spend 1s 6d on Rimmel's mahogany hair colour at the local chemist's. This of course did not go down too well at school, and, when the housecraft teacher was taking assembly, she demanded, 'What do you think you have done?' in front of the whole school. Dee also had to spend time and money straightening her naturally curly hair (with slides and clips) as curly hair was, again, not Mod.

For her first interview on leaving school, she took her mother along, but it didn't put them off. Aims of Industry in Fetter Lane in the City offered her £7 10s per week to look after the Gestetner machine and do the company's collating. With her first pay packet, she went down to Whitechapel to buy the essential (that month) Mod grey skirt and pink and grey jumper. Promotion to switchboard operator followed, and, in this new role, she changed employers to Scholl's Head office in City Road (EC1).

Now in need of extra funds for clothes and trips to the Ilford Palais, Dee took a job as a barmaid in the Queen's Head in Hackney Road. Her sister had actually been offered the job but couldn't make it, so Dee, under-age, replaced her, having told a white lie to the publican. This job, in a very busy pub with live groups, changed the way she spent her evenings completely. After working at the pub there would often be a party, or a trip to a Mod club.

When mini skirts came in, and hers were some of the shortest, she was head-hunted by the publican of the Dover Castle in Bethnal Green Road – on condition she wore her minis. She bought some mauve corduroy hot pants (c. 1968) and shortened them even further, before taking them in a carrier bag to show Alfie, the publican. With his approval, she changed into these, which proved quite a talking point with the customers. At work, she alternated between minis and maxis, which were bought in the market at the Angel (near her day job) or in Carnaby Street, the latter being the place where she bought suede hot pants with lace-up sides – one of the outfits she would never wear in front of her dad.

To hide her curls, Dee also took to wearing hairpieces, and recalls one evening, when in a clinch in a boyfriend's car near to home, her father rapped on the steamed-up windows. She had to leave in such a hurry, the hairpiece got left behind. Although the boyfriend returned it, that was the last time she saw him … but there were plenty of other fish in the sea.

# Other titles published by The History Press

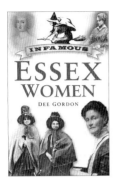

## Infamous Essex Women
DEE GORDON

From the thirteenth century onwards, Essex has produced more than its fair share of infamous women. Some got their come-uppance, some profited from their infamy and others were misguided or, with the benefit of hindsight, misjudged. The reader will find a plethora of women to hate, ridicule or secretly admire in Dee Gordon's book. Some of the characters featured here might horrify or mystify, others will provoke empathy or disbelief, but all tales are authenticated by hours of research. Read, learn, squirm – and smile!

978 0 7509 5085 5

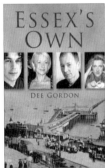

## Essex's Own
DEE GORDON

Athlete and TV presenter Sally Gunnell, painter Edward Bawden, actress Joan Sims, singer Billy Bragg, footballer Bobby Moore, chef Jamie Oliver, author John Fowles, film director Basil Dearden, playwright Sarah Kane, and the infamous highwayman Dick Turpin are among personalities through the ages who have been born in Essex. This book features mini-biographies of all these and many more, and will make fascinating reading for residents and visitors alike.

978 0 7509 5121 0

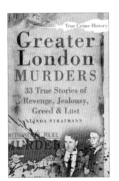

## Greater London Murders:
### 33 True Stories of Revenge, Jealousy, Greed & Lust
LINDA STRATMANN

This compendium brings together thirty-three murderous tales, including George Chapman, who was hanged in 1903 for poisoning three women; lovers Edith Thompson and Frederick Bywaters, executed for stabbing to death Thompson's husband Percy in 1922; and Donald Hume, who was found not guilty of the murder of wealthy businessman Stanley Setty in 1949, but later confessed to killing him, chopping up his body and disposing of it by aeroplane.

978 0 7524 5124 4

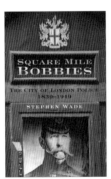

## Square Mile Bobbies: The City of London Police 1839-1949
STEPHEN WADE

*Square Mile Bobbies* is a history and casebook of the City of London police between 1839, when the force was first established after general recognition that London was not being policed effectively, and the Second World War. During this time the City police were involved in a succession of major cases, from the attempted assassination of the Rothschilds in 1862, to Jack the Ripper's brutal killing of Catherine Eddowes in 1888 and the notorious siege of Sidney Street in 1911.

978 0 7509 4952 1

Visit our website and discover thousands of other History Press books.

**www.thehistorypress.co.uk**